From 1942, when the first vehicles were delivered, until the end of the Second World War, the British Army received over 17,000 examples of the M4 Medium Tank from the United States under the Lend Lease programme. Originally given the codename *Swallow*, it was very soon after renamed *Sherman* by its new owners, in line with the British practice of naming armoured vehicles (1). This tank would become one of the most important battlefield assets in Britain's arsenal, with the possible exception of the Churchill. Indeed, General Montgomery, the overall commander of the British and Commonwealth units fighting in Normandy, considered the Sherman to be a universal tank, capable of both close infantry support and the kind of mobile warfare that would defeat the Panzers.

The Sherman served with British formations in every theatre of war including North Africa, Sicily and Italy and the Far East. But it is for the battles fought in North-western Europe — in Normandy, across Holland and finally into Germany — that the tank is probably best known. Although this book describes just a thin slice of that struggle, many aspects that apply for the complete 1939-45 period are covered. The structure of the armoured brigades and regiments is outlined in the chapter dealing with the armoured divisions as is the allocation of the different marks or types during the early stages of Operation Overlord. The role these tanks played with the regiments of the Royal Artillery and the short-lived Royal Marine Armoured Support Group is also described and although limited in scope when compared to the regiments and battalions of the Army, it is nonetheless fascinating. For those readers unfamiliar with the British military, the appendices at the end of this book may help to explain some otherwise baffling aspects. By the war's end the Sherman had served as medium tank, recovery vehicle and in a host of specialist roles. The basic design had minor modifications and the final production figures would exceed 40,000, the various models being built by eleven major manufacturers and a small army of sub-contractors. Although staggering, it should be remembered that this figure does not include the highly successful self-propelled artillery pieces and tank-destroyers which utilised the Sherman chassis. Therefore, the technical section which begins on page 59 cannot hope to be a definitive history of the development of the Sherman tank but will serve as a useful 'spotters guide' and also explain some of the terminology which is peculiarly British. In addition, many of the modifications carried out before the tanks were issued to their crews are also listed.

To avoid any unnecessary repetition, regiments or battalions are referred to by their full and correct titles, as they were during the war, when first mentioned. Following that, I have employed generally accepted abbreviations. As sources sometimes differ, I have employed the names given in *Regulations for the Clothing of the Army*, published in 1936 and the amendments published in October 1939, just weeks before the outbreak of war. When regiments or battalions are listed as part of a brigade they are shown in their order of seniority, or more correctly, precedence. This concept is explained further on page 62.

The reader should be aware that although I have used the term Firefly throughout this book to describe the Sherman tanks armed with the 17pdr anti-tank gun, it is far from certain that this term was in use during the war. It is, in fact, far more likely to be a post-war sobriquet, since accepted into general usage.

Before beginning, however, some acknowledgement of the events of June, July and August 1944 should be at least attempted.

Photographed on 1 June 1944, this Sherman III of the East Riding Yeomanry is shown reversing into a landing ship at Gosport. The AoS sign of a white 53 on a red square is clearly visible below the blue A Squadron sign on the differential housing. The tanks number, painted onto the turret side would seem to indicate a headquarters vehicle. The regiment's tank number 2, a Sherman VC Firefly, is shown on page 53.

1. The names given to Lend Lease tanks were all British inventions, many supposedly attributable to Winston Churchill. The US Army continued to refer to the Sherman as the M4 Medium Tank, its official designation, until the end of the war.

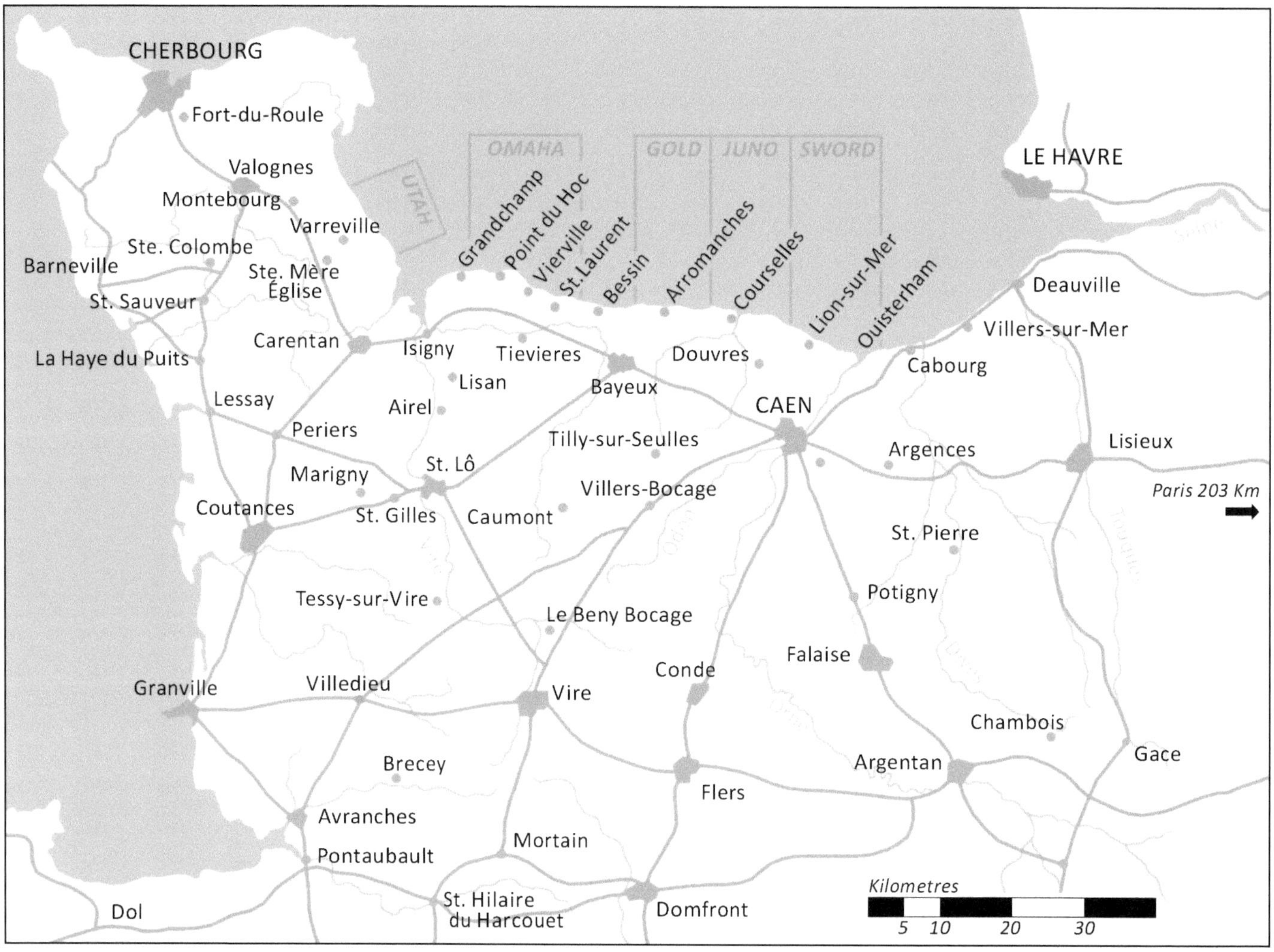

Above: Eastern and central Normandy, the invasion beaches and the Orne valley. Contemporary British and US Army maps and more recent histories give various spellings for the towns and villages shown here and even modern French sources contain anomalies. I have therefore used the names which I felt the reader would be most familiar with. The importance of the city of Caen is immediately obvious and for the British and Canadians the town would be the focus for much of the battle. The timeline below illustrates the most significant events of the campaign from the invasion until the Liberation of Paris which, officially at least, marked the end of Operation Overlord.

6 June. *British, Canadian and American troops land on the Normandy beaches as part of Operation Overlord. By the evening of the first day over 130,000 men are ashore. Although the landings are immensely successful, the town of Caen, an important road junction on the Orne river just 12 kilometres from the coast, remains in German hands as night falls. The invasion plan had called for Caen to be captured on the first day by 3rd Infantry Division of British XXX Corps and the failure to secure the town would hamper British operations until mid-July when it eventually fell.*

7 June. *The planned assault on Caen, codenamed Operation Perch, is expanded to include units of British I Corps which batters away at the German defences but is held back by constant enemy counterattacks. Hampered by the congestion on the beaches, 27th Armoured Brigade is unable to support 3rd Infantry Division's attack. Most of 7th Armoured Division is landed on this day and British XXX Corps captures Bayeux and Port-en-Bessin-Huppain.*

9 June. *US troops capture St. Mère-Église. The Luftwaffe attacks the Orne River bridges and although the Germans claim that at least one bridge is destroyed the enemy aircraft are driven off by anti-aircraft fire.*

10 June. *To the west of Caen 7th Armoured Division of XXX Corps reaches Tilly-sur-Seulles late that night and during the following morning secures the town. The planned attack by 4th Armoured Brigade and 51st (Highland) Infantry Division is postponed.*

11 June. *A determined German counterattack drives the British units from Tilly-sur-Seulles and a further attempt to reclaim the lost ground made by 50th (Northumbrian) Division is unsuccessful. An armoured assault by 2nd Canadian Armoured Brigade near Le Mesnil-Patry, almost exactly halfway between Tilly-sur-Seulles and Caen, suffers heavy casualties. On the same day units of British VIII Corps land in Normandy*

12 June. *British and US units link up at Carentan creating a continuous front. Further south, elements of 7th Armoured Division fight their way into Livry, about 20 kilometres east of St Lô. On the Allied left, the Germans launch a series of counterattacks from Breville against the Orne Bridgehead, the defence of which now takes priority over the planned advance west of Caen. Over 300,000 men and 50,000 vehicles have been landed since D-Day.*

13 June. *Units of 7th Armoured Division reach Villers-Bocage, less than 20 kilomteres to the south-west of Caen, and occupy the town by early morning. At 9.00am, without warning, the lead tanks of 4th County of London Yeomanry are attacked by a platoon of Tiger I tanks from schwere SS-Panzer-Abteilung 101 which had been observing the British troops for some time. Although the Germans are eventually driven off, 22nd Armoured Brigade has lost fourteen tanks, two anti-tank guns and a number of transport vehicles. In addition a party which had been sent east to Point 213 on the Caen road was cut off and captured. On the same day, with no sign of the Germans giving way, Operation Perch is called off.*

14 June. *7th Armoured Division is ordered to withdraw towards Caumont. US troops complete the capture of Carentan.*

25 June. *Before dawn, Operation Martlet, a limited assault made by units of British XXX Corps to capture Rauray and the German positions around Noyers west of Caen, is launched. The offensive was meant to protect the flank of Operation Epsom, which was to begin within the next 24 hours, against possible German counterattack.*

26 June. *Operation Epsom, an offensive to capture Caen by outflanking the German defenders, begins. Over the next two days a foothold is secured on the southern bank of the Odon river and expanded with units from 43rd (Wessex) Infantry Division.*

27 June. *Taking over the advance from 15th (Scottish) Division, 11th Armoured Division overruns much Hill 112, a strong German position near Caen, although the summit remains in German hands. On the same day the tanks of the Staffordshire Yeomanry and 79th Armoured Division support three regiments of 3rd Infantry Division in Operation Mitten, a limited assault to reduce a German salient based around the Chateaux of la Londe and la Landel north of Caen. The official British history dubbed this area 'the bloodiest square mile in Normandy'.*

29 June. *In anticipation of a strong counterattack all British armoured units around Hill 112 are ordered to withdraw and the hill is once again occupied by the Germans.*

30 June. *Although the expected German counterattacks are beaten off, Operation Epsom is effectively ended. Ultimately unsuccessful, Martlet and Epsom had neverthelesss inflicted heavy casualties on the German defenders, particularly the elite units of II.SS-Panzerkorps, which were now so depleted that a planned counter-offensive aimed at Bayeux was cancelled and the corps relegated to static defence. This engagement is sometimes referred to as the First Battle of the Odon. By this day over 800,000 Allied servicemen and 140,000 vehicles have been landed since the beginning of the invasion.*

1 July. *Unknown to the Allies, the Germans decide to gradually evacuate and eventually abandon Caen transferring the armoured units currently undertaking the town's defence to the west to meet the expected threat from the Americans.*

8 July. *Second Army launches Operation Charnwood, a combined British and Canadian assault to take Caen.*

9 July. *British and Canadian units enter Caen and manage to secure the northern suburbs although the Germans still hold the southern half.*

10 July. *In an effort to finally secure Hill 112 units of VIII Corps, including 4th Armoured Brigade, are ordered to attack towards the hill and capture the surrounding villages and Chateau de Fontaine in an operation codenamed Jupiter. The hill is captured on the first day after heavy fighting.*

11 July. *A German counterattack forces the British defenders from the summit of Hill 112. On the same day US troops enter St. Lô.*

15 July. *Units of British XII Corps advance towards Hill 112 and the area between Évrecy and Maizet in an operation codenamed Greenline, designed to draw the German's attention away from preparations for the upcoming Operation Goodwood. At the same time British XXX Corps commences Operation Pomegranate aimed at the high ground north-east of Villers-Bocage.*

18 July. *Operation Goodwood begins with a bombardment by over 2,000 Allied aircraft which fails to significantly damage the German defences. British VIII Corps, with the Guards, 7th and 11th Armoured Divisions, was to advance from the Orne bridgehead and capture Bretteville-sur-Laize, Vimont and Argences and head directly south towards Falaise. Importantly, VIII Corps had been ordered to destroy as many German armoured vehicles as possible. On VIII Corps' right, British I Corps was prepared for the expected German counterattacks while on the left, II Canadian Corps launched a coordinated attack codenamed Atlantic to clear the last German defenders from Caen.*

19 July. *Fighting continues in the town of Caen with the Canadians clearing the southern suburbs. 11th Armoured Division captures the hamlet of Bras and Hubert-Follie, today a suburb on the southern outskirts of Caen.*

Tanks, an Armoured Recovery Vehicle (ARV) and a jeep of 13th/18th Royal Hussars, 27th Armoured Brigade en route to Normandy. This regiment assaulted Sword Beach in support of 8th Infantry Brigade on the morning of the invasion. Note the method of securing the wading stacks to the ARV. The tank closest to the camera, named Balaclava, is also shown in the colour section on page 23.

Although the formation badge has been covered by the censor, this Sherman III almost certainly belongs to A Squadron, 24th Lancers of 8th Armoured Brigade. At this time the Lancers usually named their tanks beginning with the squadron letter and the name Armageddon has been painted in script, in the centre of the transmission cover to the right of the yellow, A Squadron sign. If our identification is correct this photograph must have been taken on 7 June 1944 when the regiment first came ashore.

20 July. *Operation Goodwood ends, in large part due to the weather, with the British armoured units holding Bourguébus Ridge some 11 kilometres from their start lines. This was the largest tank battle fought by the British Army during the Second World War.*

25 July. *The US Army's Operation Cobra begins and meets with almost immediate success. On the same day the Canadians attack German positions south of Caen as part of Operation Spring. Faced with stubborn resistance and immediate German counterattacks, the offensive stalls on the first day.*

30 July. *British troops attack Caumont, situated between St. Lô and Villers-Bocage.*

31 July. *To support Operation Cobra, British 2nd Army launches a large-scale attack codenamed Bluecoat. Both VIII and XXX Corps were to capture the important road junction of Vire and the 360-metre high Mount Pincon, both to the south-west of Caen. On the same day as the offensive begins American forces capture Avranches.*

1 August. *4th Canadian and 1st Polish Armoured Divisions arrive in Normandy*

4 August. *British units occupy Hill 112 without a fight after it has been abandoned by the Germans. With Caen gone the high ground has lost its strategic significance.*

5 August. *Infantrymen of 43rd (Wessex) Division and tanks of 13th/18th Hussars secure Mount Pinçon and are reinforced during the night, beating of a German counterattack. This action effectively brings Operation Bluecoat to an end.*

7 August. *The German's begin Operation Lüttich, a limited offensive aimed at Avranches conducted by ad-hoc battlegroups drawn from several depleted divisions.*

8 August. *Operation Totalise begins with Canadian and Polish units attacking towards Falaise in an effort to trap the German units now being pushed eastwards by the Americans. This assault saw the first use of Kangaroo armoured personnel carriers which had been converted from Priest self-propelled guns. On the same day the Americans occupy Le Mans, the headquarters of the German's 7.Armee. After some local successes the Germans are forced to call off Operation Lüttich.*

9 August. *Operation Totalise is slowed by unexpectedly stiff resistance and although Verrieres Ridge and Cintheaux are taken the Canadian and Polish units suffer high casualties.*

10 August. *Canadian units reach Hill 195, just north of Falaise.*

11 August. *The Canadian First Army calls a halt to the offensive blaming the inexperience of the armoured units for the failure and replacing them with infantry formations. In an effort to intercept the German units withdrawing after Operation Lüttich, 3rd Infantry Division and Guards Armoured Division of VIII Corps mount an attack towards Moncy on the Vire- Saint-Germain-du-Crioult road and Mont de Cerisy. In the event the attack bogs down at Le Val after gaining just 800 metres.*

14 August. *British troops launch Operation Tractable towards Falaise preceded by a massive aerial bombardment.*

17 August. *Canadian troops enter Falaise threatening the German Army in Normandy with encirclement.*

18 August. *Canadians capture Trun, 10 kilometres east of Falaise on the Argentan-Vimoutiers road.*

19 August. *During the evening elements of 1st Polish Armoured Division link up with US troops at Chambois just south of Mount Ormel.*

20 August. *A German counterattack manages to reopen the corridor to the Falaise Pocket allowing thousands of trapped German troops to escape.*

21 August. *During the early evening Polish and Canadian troops meet at Coudehard, north-east of Trun, closing the German escape route for the last time.*

23 August. *The first Allied units enter Paris.*

25 August. *Paris, the final objective of Operation Overlord, is liberated.*

30 August. *The last German troops cross the Seine. The battle for Normandy is over.*

The British Army fought the Normandy battles with four armoured divisions, four independent armoured brigades and three independent tank brigades. The latter were mainly equipped with Churchill tanks and were intended to support the infantry in breaking through the enemy's frontline defences. Although each did operate a handful of Sherman tanks they are only examined here briefly and it is only necessary to mention that they were organised in a similar fashion to the armoured brigades. Other armoured units included self-propelled artillery and anti-tank regiments, the Airborne Reconnaissance Regiment and formations equipped with armoured cars such as the regiments of the Reconnaissance Corps, the RAF Regiment, the 21st Army and the four Corps protection troops. These, however, with the exception of some artillery units, were not equipped with the Sherman or any of its variants and although interesting, fall outside the area of our study. The following is an explanation of the formation and organisation of the relevant formations with brief operational histories of their involvement in the Normandy battles. As many readers may find certain aspects of the British military confusing, if not completely bewildering, a section is included on page 62 which endeavours to explain certain terms and customs such as the origins of the Royal Armoured Corps, the naming and numbering of battalions and regiments and the subject of seniority.

THE ARMOURED DIVISIONS

The British armoured division of 1944 had evolved through the hard lessons of the disastrous battles of 1940, the North African campaign and the fighting in Sicily and Italy, both of which included amphibious operations. At the time of the Normandy landings each division contained an armoured brigade made up of a brigade headquarters, three armoured regiments and a motor battalion of infantry transported in armoured halftracks. Each armoured regiment comprised a headquarters squadron and three tank squadrons referred to as A, B and C squadrons. The squadrons were usually commanded by a major and, officially at least, consisted of two tanks. The squadron headquarters also controlled any armoured recovery vehicles (ARV) or close-support (CS) tanks. By June 1944 the fighting, or Sabre, squadrons were divided into five, or sometimes four, troops and these were numbered sequentially throughout the regiment (1). The official establishment for each troop was four tanks, one of which was supposed to be a Sherman Firefly armed with the lethal 17pdr anti-tank gun, but in practice this number could vary.

Below: Several interesting features are visible on this Sherman V Artillery Observation Post (OP) tank including the tactical marking identifying the second battery of an artillery regiment in front of the lap gunner's position with, to the left, the conical-shaped No.10 antenna mount which was an identifying feature of command and OP tanks. Just visible on the hull glacis as a slightly darker oval in front of the driver's position is a patch of poison gas detection paint. Note the waterproofing behind the driver and that the barrel is not a dummy. This photograph is taken from a series depicting 76th Highland Field Regiment, Royal Artillery made just prior to the invasion.

1. The organisational changes to the standard armoured brigade operating in the UK, of both August 1942 and November 1943, called for an armoured squadron of five troops. However, there is evidence that many armoured squadrons fighting in Normandy contained only four troops and that this establishment was common would seem to be confirmed by the allocation in June 1944 of thirty-six 17pdr armed tanks each to the Guards, 7th and 11th Armoured Divisions and 4th Armoured Brigade. As the normal practice at that time was to field one Firefly per troop, this would mean that those units had a full complement if the squadrons were made up from four troops. Within 27th Armoured Brigade the squadrons of the Staffordshire Yeomanry were definitely organised with four troops and probably East Riding Yeomanry while 13th/18th Hussars' A and B Squadrons retained the five-troop structure while C Squadron contained four troops. That some localised experimentation was condoned is borne out by the account of an officer of 3 RTR who states that prior to D-Day his battalion had concentrated all its Fireflies into a single troop but reverted to the official establishment before leaving Britain.

21st Army Group Tank Strength June 1944 - Sherman tanks

	I	II	III	V	IC	VC	I OP	II OP	III OP	V OP	II DD	V DD	III ARV	V ARV	V Crab
Guards Armoured Division				157		36				8				11	
7th Armoured Division						36									
11th Armoured Division				157		36				8				11	
79th Armoured Division															
30th Armoured Brigade *				72										12	180
1st Army Tank Brigade	50	27					8							6	
4th Armoured Brigade		157				36		8						11	
8th Armoured Brigade			95			22			8		76		9	2	
27th Armoured Brigade			126			29			8			38	9	2	
33rd Armoured Brigade	157					36	8							11	
6th Guards Tank Brigade				4											
31st Tank Brigade				4											
34th Tank Brigade				4											
15th/19th Hussars **												75			
4th Canadian Armoured Division				225		36				8				14	
2nd Canadian Armoured Brigade			95			22			8			76	9	2	
1st Polish Armoured Division				139	2	23				5				11	
Armoured Replacement Group	52	50	150	178		24								12	45

All vehicles are listed by their British designations, for example V is Sherman V or M4A4, III is Sherman III or M4A2. The letter C identifies a 17pdr armed tank, OP denotes Observation Post, DD is Duplex Drive, ARV is Armoured Recovery Vehicle and the Crabs are of course the tanks fitted with the mine-clearing flail. Note that these figures are taken from Royal Armoured Corps reports and do not include OP tanks attached to Royal Artillery regiments, ARV tanks of the Corps of Engineers or the command tanks of the Royal Marine batteries. Although not part of our study, the numbers for the Canadian and Polish units are included.

** Exactly half of the seventy-two Sherman V tanks allocated to 30th Armoured Brigade are listed as Pilot tanks with a mention of twelve Roller equipments being on hand. A Sherman V photographed near Les Thilliers-en-Vexin in late August, quite probably of 79th Armoured Division, has the brackets necessary to fit the Canadian Indestructible Roller Device (CIRD) and this may be one of the tanks listed here.*

*** In June 1944, 15th/19th King's Royal Hussars were still in Britain. In early August the regiment replaced 2nd Northamptonshire Yeomanry as the reconnaissance regiment of 11th Armoured Division and relinquished their Shermans for Cromwells.*

I have been unable to discover much further information regarding the Sherman V tanks allocated to the Guards, 31st and 34th Tank Brigades. The November 1943 Tank Brigade organisation calls for four Cruiser tanks for the brigade headquarters and Nafziger has four Sherman V command tanks attached to a combat group directly under headquarters command with a number of Churchill OP tanks and the brigade's Crusader AA vehicles. There is, however, evidence of one of the Guards Shermans operating with the 3rd Battallion Scots Guards, the brigade's junior regiment, suggesting that the four tanks were spread between the brigade and regimental commands.

The allocation of Fireflies was by no means complete when the first landings took place, with some regiments receiving their allocation as late as 28 May 1944, just over one week prior to the invasion. As production increased some troops were able to field more than one Firefly and by the end of the fighting on the Western Front it was not unusual to find at least two of these powerful tanks in each troop.

The close-support tanks, armed with the 95mm howitzer, were removed from the Sherman squadrons and retained only with those regiments operating Cromwell tanks. This was, in all likelihood, due to the Sherman tank's ability to fire both armour-piercing and high-explosive rounds, eliminating the need for a specialised tank (1).

The overall command of the armoured regiment was exercised by a Lieutenant-Colonel and the regimental headquarters fielded four tanks: one each for the commanding officer, the second in command, the adjutant and the Regimental Sergeant Major. The regimental headquarters squadron controlled a reconnaissance troop of eleven Stuart light tanks and a communications troop, referred to as a Link Troop. The latter was essentially an armoured taxi service and contained nine Humber or Daimler scout cars, one of which was usually reserved for the regimental commander. Although not strictly relevant to this study, mention should be made of the anti-aircraft troop equipped with Crusader AA tanks attached to each armoured regiment at the beginning of thecampaign. These quickly became redundant and although some regiments retained theirs, a great many AA units were converted to infantry, their vehicles being used as Observation Post (OP) tanks.

In addition to the tank regiments, the armoured divisions also contained an armoured reconnaissance regiment equipped with Cromwell and Stuart tanks. As the burden of the scouting and reconnaissance role was actually carried out by the Corps armoured car regiments or by the Stuart tanks of the regimental reconnaissance troop, these units effectively provided the brigade with a fourth armoured regiment.

The division's artillery was controlled by a Brigadier referred to as Commander, Royal Artillery (CRA) and each of the armoured divisions had two field regiments, an anti-tank regiment and an anti-aircraft regiment. A number of these were equipped with Sherman OP tanks and are discussed further under the heading of the individual regiment.

1. The exact reasoning is unknown and in fact the close-support concept was retained by the British until the war's end in Italy with the Sherman IB, armed with the 105mm howitzer, filling the role. It is possible that maintaining both the Cromwell and Sherman within the same unit was thought to be too much of a logistical strain although there is anecdotal evidence that at least some Polish and Canadian Sherman squadrons operating in France retained their CS tanks as the Canadian units later transferred from Italy certainly did.

Guards Armoured Division. Formed in May 1941, in the expectation that this formation would be used to repel a German invasion, the division originally contained 5th and 6th Guards Armoured Brigades. In late 1942, 6th Guards Armoured Brigade was detached and would eventually be equipped with Churchill tanks and re-organised as an independent tank brigade. The remaining brigade retained its original title and was made up of 2nd Armoured Battalion Grenadier Guards, 1st Armoured Battalion Coldstream Guards and 2nd Armoured Battalion Irish Guards. The men of the 1st Battalion Grenadier Guards formed the brigade's motor battalion (1). The reconnaissance regiment was 2nd Armoured Battalion Welsh Guards equipped with Cromwell tanks including the CS version.

The brigade was at first equipped with Covenanter tanks but completed much of its training with the Crusader. During 1943 the cruiser tanks were replaced by American M4 Medium tanks and by early 1944 the armoured regiments were equipped with the Sherman V, the M4A4, throughout. In deference to their origins as guardians of the monarch, the armoured units continued to be referred to by the infantry titles of battalion, instead of regiment, and company, in place of squadron. Elements of the division began landing in France on 26 June 1944 and soon after arriving in Normandy took part in the fighting around Carpiquet airfield coming up against elements of 12.SS-Panzer-Division, although these actions were little more than skirmishes and much of the division's tanks were still being ferried across the Channel from Britain.

On 18 July, together with 7th and 11th Armoured Divisions, the complete division took part in Operation Goodwood, the latest in a series of attempts to seize the city of Caen on the Orne river some 15 kilometres from the invasion beaches. The offensive was originally planned as a combined arms operation but due to the unexpectedly high casualty rate within infantry formations the attack was largely carried out by armoured units. The Guards were to advance towards Vimont and Argences, just to the east of Caen, and push on to Cagny. They soon came up against stiff German resistance including a battery of Luftwaffe 88mm anti-tank guns dug into prepared defensive positions and although the fire from these guns could prove devastating it is unlikely that they managed to account for the destruction of sixty of the Guards' tanks as is claimed in some accounts with the division reporting the loss of fifteen tanks destroyed and forty-five tanks damaged for the entire operation. Indeed, the 88mm guns did considerable damage to a counterattack made later by elements of 21.Panzer-Division and Tiger tanks from schwere Panzer-Abteilung 503 when they failed to recognise their comrades and destroyed at least two Tigers.

The fighting continued for the remainder of the day and its desperate nature can be gauged by the action involving Lieutenant John Gorman, a troop commander with the Irish Guards. Probing towards

Photographed in the streets of Villiers-Bretonneux sometime after the breakout from Normandy this image provides a good impression of the appearance of the Sherman V tanks of the Guards Armoured Division throughout the campaign. The Guards' formation badge is clearly visible on the transmission cover below the driver's position. To the left, the white number 51 on a red square identifies the senior regiment of an armoured brigade, in this case 2nd Armoured Battalion Grenadier Guards. This regiment did not use squadron signs and instead numbered their tanks sequentially and this vehicle's number is marked in white on the hull side.

1. The Grenadiers had been allotted this role as the battalion contained the King's Company, made up of Guardsmen who were all over six foot tall and for obvious reasons could not be expected to climb into and out of the restrictive spaces of a tank.

Sherman V tanks of 2nd Armoured Battalion Irish Guards during the advance south of Caumont at the beginning of July. The tank's name, Clochan, can be seen painted in white just in front of the driver. The formation badge of the Guards Division can be seen on the right of the transmission cover and the AoS of the junior armoured regiment, a white 53 on a red square, is on the left. A 3rd Squadron sign enclosing a number 2 is painted on the hull side between the pieces of applique armour, an identifying feature of this regiment.

A Sherman V followed by a VC Firefly of 1st Armoured Battalion Coldstream Guards passing through Fouilloy on their way to Arras after the breakout from Normandy. The replacement of the large .50 cal machinegun with the smaller and lighter .30 cal was common in British armoured regiments by this time. Note that lengths of Churchill track have been attached to the turret of the nearest tank.

Cagny, today less than 2 kilometres from the outer suburbs of Caen, Lieutenant Gorman with the Shermans of his troop came upon a number of German tanks including at least one Tiger II and a Tiger I. Opening fire immediately, the first round from the Gorman's 75mm gun bounced harmlessly off the Tiger II and finding that his tank's gun was now jammed Gorman ordered his driver to ram the German tank. This, and the fire from the remaining Shermans, convinced the Tiger crew to abandon their tank and the other Germans also retreated. Early that evening, after beating off another counterattack by tanks of the Tiger battalion, infantry units entered Cagny only to find the village completely empty.

Sporadic fighting continued into the night, with the Luftwaffe making a rare appearance, and resumed the next day and, although the Guards managed to reach the ridge at Bourgebus, the British divisions were unable to advance much further and held little more than the ground they had taken by lunch time on the first day.

Almost immediately following Goodwood the division was reorganised into separate battlegroups consisting of 2nd Armoured Battalion Grenadier Guards with the Grenadiers of 1st Motor Battalion and referred to as the Grenadier Group, while 2nd Armoured Battalion Irish Guards were paired with 3rd Battalion Irish Guards and known as the Irish group. The tanks of 1st Armoured Battalion Coldstream Guards supported 5th Battalion Coldstream Guards and were called the Coldstream Group. There is some suggestion that 1st Armoured Battalion Coldstream Guards also operated with 1st Battalion Welsh Guards and this could be true as the system was intended to be flexible (1). Each group was allocated a battery of Sexton self-propelled guns from 153rd (Leicestershire Yeomanry) Field Regiment with 129 Battery, 130 Battery and 131 Battery supporting the Irish, Grenadier and Coldstream groups respectively.

In early August the division took part in Operation Bluecoat, the attempt to capture the town of Vire, to the west and south of Caen, and secure the area around Mount Pinçon. It was hoped that this assault would exploit the success of the Americans' Operation Cobra which had begun a week earlier and also strike the Germans at a point where they had not been able to concentrate their armour, much of which now lay about Caen.

Initially the Guards, under the command of VIII Corps, were deployed on the flank of 11th Armoured Division which spearheaded the assault, however, after just two days of fighting the division took the lead role.

The division remained in this area and when the Germans withdrew towards Falaise were given a few days to rest and refit. On Sunday, 27 August the division was transferred to XXX Corps and took part in the advance to the Seine reaching the river by the following Tuesday, meeting almost no resistance.

A military policeman of 3rd Infanrty Division controls traffic as a Sherman V of the Coldstream Guards, the second senior regiment of 5th Guards Armoured Brigade, moves forward for the start of Operation Goodwood on 18 July 1944. The Guard's formation badge can be seen on the left of the hull at the rear and the AoS sign on the right. Of note is the attachment of pieces of the sandshield to the rear hull as stowage bins, a practice more commonly seen on the Sherman tanks of 4th and 22nd Armoured Brigades – the North African veterans.

1. There are several conflicting accounts and the arrangement detailed here was taken in part from Fitzgerald's history of the Irish Guards and the account of the Leicestershire Yeomanry association.

7th Armoured Division. Better known as the Desert Rats, this formation could trace its origins to the Mobile Force raised prior to the outbreak of war from garrison troops in Egypt. The title 7th Armoured Division was first introduced on 16 February 1940.

Most of the division had arrived in France by 8 June 1944 and at that time the armoured element was provided by 22nd Armoured Brigade. The brigade contained 1st Royal Tank Regiment, 5th Royal Tank Regiment and 4th County of London Yeomanry with the 1st Battalion, The Rifle Brigade making up the motor battalion. Together with the division's reconnaissance regiment, 8th King's Royal Irish Hussars, all these units had served in the North African campaign.

The regiments of 22nd Armoured Brigade were equipped with Cromwell tanks, supported by one Sherman Firefly per troop, although there is anecdotal evidence that suggests 1st Royal Tank Regiment had one extra Firefly on hand in June 1944. As with most armoured units the proportion of 17pdr tanks increased as these became available with the number on hand rising from thirty-six in June 1944 to sixty-seven by the end of the year. On 13 June 1944, during Operation Perch, 4th County of London Yeomanry suffered severe losses after being surprised by an enemy force in the town of Villers-Bocage. Indeed, the regiment was so badly mauled in this and subsequent actions that it was eventually amalgamated with 3rd County of London Yeomanry of 4th Armoured Brigade from 29 July 1944, becoming 3rd/4th County of London Yeomanry. The regiment was soon replaced by 5th Royal Inniskilling Dragoon Guards, which then became the senior regiment of the brigade.

Following the action at Villers-Bocage the division withdrew to the west of the town to an area of higher ground between Amayé-sur-Seulles and St-Germain-d'Ectot expecting that 50th (Northumbrian) Infantry Division was moving towards their position. By nightfall, however, they found themselves completely exposed and in danger of being cut off. As they would have done in the Desert, they formed a square or box with 1st Royal Tank Regiment covering the road north to Livry, 5th Royal Tank Regiment securing the eastern and western flanks and the survivors of 4th County of London Yeomanry positioned in Amayé-sur-Seulles close to the brigade headquarters. The

A Sherman VC Firefly coming ashore on 7 June 1977 from a LST (Landing Ship, Tank) on Sword Beach. Although no markings can be seen, other than a bridging classification indicating the tank's weight class, the authorised regimental history attributes this tank to the 3rd County of London Yeomanry. Note the waterproof on the main gun and the temporary loading numbers on the front right fender which indicate the craft to which the vehicle is allocated and its place on the ship.

A heavily camouflaged Sherman VC Firefly, followed by a Cromwell, photographed after crossing London Bridge over the Orne River at the start of Operation Goodwood on 18 July 1944. In the original print of this image the Royal Tank Regiment cap badge worn by the crew of the Firefly is clearly visible as is the 7th Armoured Division formation badge worn by the Cromwell commander indicating that this is either 1st or 5th Royal Tank regiment of 22nd Armoured Brigade.

guns 5th Royal Horse Artillery, which would play a crucial role in the coming fight, were stationed along the northern edge of the perimeter. Some assistance was provided by US 1st Infantry Division whose forward observers at Caumont were able to call in artillery support until the Germans were too close to the British positions. In the early hours of 14 June, after an initial probe that was broken up by artillery fire, the Germans attacked in strength. Throughout the morning German Grenadiers were thrown at the British lines and at one point overran a platoon of infantry and penetrated the British position only to be ejected by a strong counterattack made by tanks.

Exchanges of rifle and machine gun fire continued into the afternoon until, at 2.00pm, mortar rounds began falling on the British defenders followed by artillery fire which gradually grew in intensity. At 5.00pm the Germans launched a two pronged attack from the north and south supported by tanks which almost reached the brigade headquarters before being beaten back sometime after 10.00pm. Although the commander of 22nd Armoured Brigade was confident of holding the position, he was ordered to retreat and, using the cover provided by the noise of a nearby bombing raid, all units withdrew shortly after midnight. Although technically a part of Operation Perch, the division's history refers to this action as the Battle of the Box.

Further operations were scheduled but the lack of supplies and reinforcements arriving from the beaches meant that the division spent the next few weeks in refitting. On 18 July, together with the Guards and 11th Armoured Divisions, the division took part in Operation Goodwood with 5th Royal Tank Regiment capturing the town of Bourguébus at the foot of the ridge outside Caen despite heavy shelling and the chaos caused by the congested roads along the assault routes. At the same time 4th County of London Yeomanry, which had yet to leave the division, reached Bras on the Caen-Falaise road. The overall gains were meagre however and when the offensive was called off, due to the torrential rain, the division was forced to hold the positions in front of Bourguébus Ridge.

On 29 July, 7th Armoured Division, as part of XXX Corps, took part in Operation Spring in support of 2nd Canadian Corps. This was the last action in which 4th County of London Yeomanry would fight with the division and the regiment's remaining Fireflies destroyed five German tanks and a number of self-propelled guns. In the early morning hours of Tuesday, 1 August, with 5th Royal Tank Regiment in the lead, the division advanced towards Aunay-sur-Audon, south of Villers-Bocage, as part of Operation Bluecoat.

By Thursday little headway had been made and that afternoon the lead tanks were hit by a strong German counterattack mounted by infantry with armoured support including a number of Tiger and Panther tanks. In the fighting that followed the British infantry suffered heavily and A and B Squadrons of 5th Royal Tank Regiment were almost completely destroyed. Further progress was stalled by an extensive minefield, but by 6th August, 5th Iniskilling Dragoon Guards had reached Mount Pinçon, a major objective of the operation, and supported the infantry of 1/7th Battalion Queen's Royal Regiment who had managed to gain a foothold on the plateau after attacking in complete darkness. At the same time units of 43rd (Wessex) Division and Sherman tanks of 13th/18th Hussars had worked their way to the summit along an old farm track, much to the surprise of the defenders. Although the Germans mounted a counterattack the next morning, it was something of a half-hearted attempt and they were driven off by the guns of the Royal Horse Artillery.

Later that day the XXX Corps commander, Lieutenant General Brian Horrocks, established his headquarters on the top off Mont Pinçon and immediately ordered an attack towards Condé-sur-Noireau on the Caen-Flers road some 12 kilometres distant. The lead column ran into difficulties from the start in the thick Bocage country and the attack was called off.

Following Bluecoat, much of the division was withdrawn to Aunay, although the Iniskilling Dragoons remained at the front supporting units of 43rd Infantry Division.

On 17 August, with the German defenders of Normandy either fighting desperately to avoid encirclement in the Falaise Pocket or retreating towards the east, 7th Armoured Division was sent towards the Seine and reached Livarot on the River Vie on the following day. By 20 August the division's engineers had constructed a bridge over the river that could support 22nd Armoured Brigade's tanks and on the next day, as the German's last escape route from Falaise was closed, the Touques river was crossed after a bridge was captured intact (1).

By this time the Germans were simply unable to counterattack with their customary decisiveness and aggression and although local defensive operations were mounted by small, often isolated, groups of infantry and one or two tanks, the Allies increasingly found that they were able to brush these aside. The garrison of Lisieux surrendered on 23 August after an assault by 1/6th Battalion Queen's Royal Regiment and the Iniskilling Dragoons. Skirting the town the division continued its advance and by the evening of 28 August had reached the Seine near the Forêt Domaniale de Brotonne, 15 kilometres west of Rouen.

After the successful conclusion of Operation Overlord The division soldiered on with 21st Army Group, taking part in the liberation of Belgium, the Netherlands and northern Germany.

A Sherman Artillery Observation Post (AOP) tank of 3rd Regiment Royal Horse Artillery and a Cromwell photographed in Doullens during the division's drive to the Seine. A combined 7th Armoured Division formation badge and AoS sign of a white 74 on a red over blue square, denoting the senior Field Artillery Regiment of an armoured division, can be seen in front of the lap gunner's position. In front of the driver's hatch is a similar square with a white Z indicating RHQ. The division's Desert Rat formation badge has been repeated just under the hull machine gun.

1. Although the narrative is unclear, this must have been the bridge in front of Saint-Martin-de-la-Lieue, less than 3 kilometres south of Lisieux, as it is the only place where the road north crosses the river.

11th Armoured Division. Considered by many military historians to be the best British armoured formation to have served in North-western Europe, the division's 29th Armoured Brigade was made up of 23rd Hussars, 3rd Royal Tank Regiment and 2nd Fife and Forfar Yeomanry. The reconnaissance regiment, 2nd Northamptonshire Yeomanry, was replaced on 8 August by 15th/19th The King's Royal Hussars.

The first units arrived in Normandy a week after the initial landings and on 26 June, the division was committed to Operation Epsom under the command of VII Corps. With the Cromwell tanks of the Northants Yeomanry in the lead, the division moved off in the early afternoon with the task of reaching the Odon river. Very soon however the regiments of 29th Armoured Brigade were involved in several confusing actions around Cheux and the airfield at Carpiquet, becoming entangled in the thick Bocage countryside as a consequence and also losing a number of tanks. To add to the general turmoil, the other units of VIII Corps, including 4th Armoured Brigade, were moving along the same restrictive roads. The next day the Sherman tanks of the Fife and Forfar Yeomanry fought to capture intact the bridge at Grainville-sur-Odon and 23rd Hussars managed to advance past the road from Caen to Villers-Bocage between Mouen and Mondrainville and reach the Odon. Although they had no means by which to cross the river, the tanks continued to fire at the German defenders on the opposite bank. Late in the afternoon an infantry regiment of 15th (Scottish) Division was able to secure the bridge at Tourmauville, south of Tourville-sur-Odon, and by 7.00pm two squadrons of 23rd Hussars had been pushed across the river.

They were able to secure the bridge at Tourmauville, south of Tourville-sur-Odon, and by 7.00pm two squadrons of 23rd Hussars had been pushed across.

On 28 June the tanks of 23rd Hussars, with infantrymen from the brigade's motor battalion, fought all day to take Hill 112, situated halfway between Évrecy and Baron-sur-Odon, a feature so prominent in the flat Norman countryside that it could be seen from the invasion beaches. Although the summit was captured and a strong German counterattack beaten back, the British units on the hill found themselves surrounded on three sides. The tank crews of the 23rd Hussars were exhausted and were replaced by 3rd Royal Tank Regiment late in the day. Early on the following day, 29 June, the Germans counterattacked all along the corridor leading to Hill 112 and the decision was made to abandon the position. On 30 June the tanks of the division fought off a number of counterattacks on what was by now called the Odon Bridgehead and the infantrymen of the Rifle Brigade once again managed to reach the summit of Hill 112, only to be ordered to withdraw the next morning.

The commander of the German forces in France considered Hill 112 to be the key to Caen and by extension the Normandy battlefield and would have been prepared to accept almost any price to retake it. That the British had failed to grasp its significance is astounding and they were to pay dearly for its eventual capture.

As part of Operation Goodwood, which commenced on 18 July, 11th Armoured Division led the advance to the Bourguébus Ridge, west of Caen, with the Guards and 7th Armoured Divisions. Once again

The commanding officer of 11th Armoured Division, Major General G.P.B. 'Pip' Roberts, with Brigadier Roscoe Harvey, commander of 29th Armoured Brigade, photographed in front of Harvey's Sherman V command tank. The vehicle is also shown in the illustration section on page 19.

Sherman V gun tanks of 2nd Fife and Forfar Yeomanry, the junior armoured regiment of 11th Armoured Division's 29th Armoured Brigade, photographed as they pass through Bayeaux on 8 June 1944. The blue A Squadron sign can be seen on the hull side and at the centre of the transmission cover, unusually rendered as a solid shape. The name painted at the centre of the transmission cover is unfortunately indecipherable.

the tanks of 29th Armoured Brigade ran into stiff resistance with the Fife and Forfar Yeomanry losing a complete squadron in a single action in front of the village of Cagny on the Caen-Vimont road. Although 3rd Royal Tank Regiment bypassed Cagny and reached Hubert-Follie, the tanks came up against a formidable defensive line which included a number of dug-in 88mm guns backed up by tanks and assault guns and could go no further. By the end of the day the regiment had five operational tanks.

The squadrons of 2nd Fife and Forfar Yeomanry then attempted to break through the German position west of Soliers, aiming at the village of Bourguébus which lay just beyond, but were also halted. A further attack on the same defences made by the 23rd Hussars met with an equal lack of success and in desperation the division's commander, General 'Pip' Roberts, ordered the Cromwells of the 2nd Northamptonshire Yeomanry forward. Unknown to the British tankers a number of Panther tanks had just arrived to reinforce the German position and these had little difficulty in stopping the Cromwells. Undeterred, Roberts ordered his tanks back into action on the following morning and this time 2nd Northamptonshire Yeomanry smashed their way into Bras with the Shermans of 2nd Fife and Forfar Yeomanry taking Hubert-Follie. By the end of the day the division occupied positions on the ridge. Although material losses in this battle were considerable, they could be easily replaced and losses in personnel were relatively light, particularly when measured against the gains made.

Following the experience gained in the Epsom and Goodwood battles the division was organised into four battlegroups formed from 29th Armoured Brigade and the division's 159th Infantry Brigade. The Sherman tanks of 23rd Hussars were supported by 3rd Battalion Monmouthshire Regiment, 2nd Fife and Forfar Yeomanry with 4th Battalion King's Shropshire Light Infantry and 3rd Royal Tank Regiment and 1st Battalion Herefordshire Regiment. The Cromwell-equipped 2nd Northamptonshire Yeomanry was paired with 8th Battalion The Rifle Brigade which had been the motor rifle regiment of 29th Armoured Brigade. This arrangement would last until the end of the war.

On 30 July, Operation Bluecoat was launched and the division was tasked with protecting the flank of the 6th Guards Tank Brigade and 15th Scottish Division. Although the attack started badly, the division managed to take all its objectives and by the time darkness fell had advanced as far as the road from Caumont to St Martin. On the following day the Fife and Forfar Yeomanry secured St Martin before midday and the Northamptonshire Yeomanry group stumbled upon an unguarded road and followed it all the way to Le Bény-Bocage, north-east of Vire, capturing the bridge over the Soulevre river without sustaining a single casualty. The capture of the Soulevre bridge allowed the division's battlegroups to penetrate the German defences and the remaining days of the operation were characterised by confused encounter battles with the British units finally adopting defensive positions to hold the gains they had made. In addition to the territory gained, Operation Bluecoat had held down some of the best units available to the Germans when they were sorely needed to counter the US Army's Operation Cobra. The division was severely depleted however and 2nd Northamptonshire Yeomanry was disbanded with the survivors going to 1st Northamptonshire Yeomanry and 7th Armoured Division.

After Normandy, 11th Armoured Division took part in the advance to Amiens, known as the Great Swan, the liberation of Antwerp, Operation Market Garden and also fought in the Ardennes. By the end of the war he division stood on the Danish border.

Another photograph of Brigadier Harvey's command Sherman V taken just before the start of Operation Epsom on 26 June 1944. Note what are apparently steps welded to the transmission cover and the left side fender which is missing in the image on page 13.

Sherman V tanks of 11th Armoured Division, possibly 3rd Royal Tank Regiment, pause next to a 6pdr anti-tank gun and a collection of German prisoners in St Charles-de-Percy, on the road to Vire on 2 August 1944.

79th Armoured Division. This division took part in every major engagement, and many minor battles, of the North-west Europe campaign under the leadership of its brilliant and innovative commander Major General Sir Percy Hobart. The division's armoured vehicles were modified for specialist roles, such as mine-clearing and bunker busting, and it was never intended to fight as a regular armoured formation. Rather, the division's purpose was purely tactical and as such its brigades were self-supporting, with regiments or individual squadrons being detached as required. Consequently the division had no organic infantry or artillery units. In June 1944, the commander of 79th Armoured Division was directly responsible to 21st Army Group headquarters and the division's organisation and equipment reflected its unique mission. The specialised armoured vehicles were for the most part based on the British Churchill and American M4 Sherman and M3 Grant tanks. A complete examination of the vehicles used by this division is far beyond the scope of this book and I will only discuss the Sherman-equipped units

30th Armoured Brigade. Made up of the 22nd Dragoons, with the 1st Lothians and Border Horse and the 2nd County of London Yeomanry (The Westminster Dragoons). This brigade operated Sherman Crab Flail tanks. Each regiment consisted of a headquarters equipped with three Sherman V gun tanks and a Sherman Armoured Recovery Vehicle (ARV). The regiment's three squadrons each contained a headquarters with three Sherman V tanks and was made up of four Crab troops each with five flail tanks. The squadron also contained a Pilot Troop with four Sherman gun tanks and these may have been adapted to carry the Canadian Indestructible Roller Device (CIRD) although it is doubtful that many, if any, were fitted. An RAC report of June 1944 mentions that all Crab conversions were based on Sherman V tanks.

1st Army Tank Brigade. Comprising 11th Royal Tank Regiment, 42nd Royal Tank Regiment and 49th Royal Tank Regiment in June 1944 this brigade was principally equipped with the Canal Defence Light (CDL) based on the US M3 Grant tank. The name CDL was intentionally confusing as this was considered a secret weapon. The tank's turret armament was removed and replaced with a powerful carbon-arc searchlight which was intended to not only illuminate the battlefield at night for friendly forces but would also blind or at least disorient the enemy. In addition to the CDL vehicles the brigade had a number of Sherman tanks on hand. The brigade headquarters was allocated eight Sherman OP tanks and it is almost certain that these are the Sherman I OP vehicles listed in the June 1944 RAC return. Each of the brigade's battalions was made up of a headquarters with four Sherman gun tanks and each of the battalion's three squadrons contained a squadron headquarters with three Sherman tanks and one Sherman ARV. The squadrons contained three troops, each with two Sherman tanks and six Grant CDL tanks. At least one source states that the Shermans allocated to each troop to provide protection for the CDL tanks were Sherman II models although it seems more likely that these were allocated to the squadron headquarters as twenty-seven was the exact number required. The number of tanks actually with the troops is four short of the authorised total of fifty-four and there are also three less Sherman ARV than the official allocation would allow suggesting that just two were attached to each battalion. Nevertheless, I feel it is reasonable to assume that the fifty Sherman I tanks were distributed at troop level.

The division also contained 1st Assault Brigade, Royal Engineers equipped with Churchill Infantry tanks armed with the 290mm Petard mortar and supported by Assault Park Squadron and 87th Assault Dozer squadron.

Sherman Crab flail tanks of 30th Armoured Brigade photographed with tanks and other vehicles of the Staffordshire Yeomanry on 18 July 1944. The .50 cal machine gun of the Crab has been replaced with the M3 smoke mortar that was usually fixed inside the turret to fire forward. The large turret number, common in this brigade, and name on the hull side of the of the Crab at right are unfortunately obscured by stowage and extra equipment.

Above: 1. The Royal Artillery tactical sign identifying the commander of of an artillery regiment's 2nd Battery. 2. The Arm of Service sign (AoS) denoting the second field artillery regiment attached to an armoured division. 3. The Guards Armoured Division formation badge. Most, if not all, the division's vehicles carried this marking, some with slight variations.

Above: Sherman V AOP. 153rd (Leicestershire Yeomanry) Field Regiment, RA,Guards Armoured Division. June 1944. Fitted for deep wading, this tank has the 'Houseboat' fittings on the hull sides and on the glacis. 'Houseboat' was the codename for a large rigid canvas cover which was intended to make the tank appear to be a lorry. Note the Bofors 40mm ammunition box welded to the hull side, painted in SCC 2. The marking on the wading stack may be some kind of depth indicator.

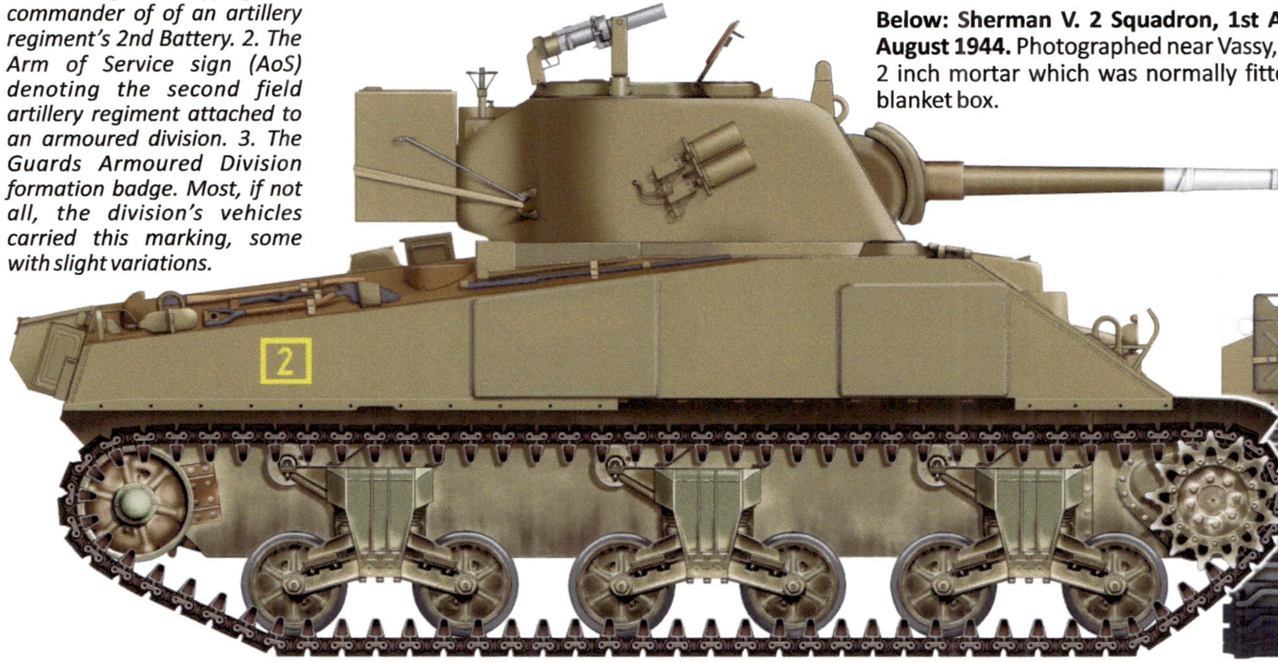

Below: Sherman V. 2 Squadron, 1st Armoured Battalion Coldstream Guards, Guards Armoured Division. August 1944. Photographed near Vassy, the machine gun of the commander's hatch has been replaced with the 2 inch mortar which was normally fitted internally. Of note are the turret smoke dischargers and the large blanket box.

In addition to the squadron sign and troop number the Coldstream Guards tanks used a system of numbering where the troop number was followed by a letter identifying the individual tank. For example, 2 would be the 2 Troop commander, 2A for the second tank of the troop and so on. These were almost always found on the rear of the blanket box. Note also the 2 Squadron sign that has been repeated on the rear hull stowage box and the number 52 AoS sign identifying the second senior regiment of an armoured brigade. The white-painted barrel is quite unusual on a 75mm gun.

The painting of the 17pdr barrel in an effort to conceal or disguise it, is thought to have first been suggested by Rex Whistler, a pre-war artist and officer of the Welsh Guards who was killed on 18 July 1944. This is, however, the only example of its use during the Normandy battles that I have been able to verify from photographs (1) and it may be that the more elaborate painting or counter-shading schemes (2) did not come into common use until the autumn at least.

1

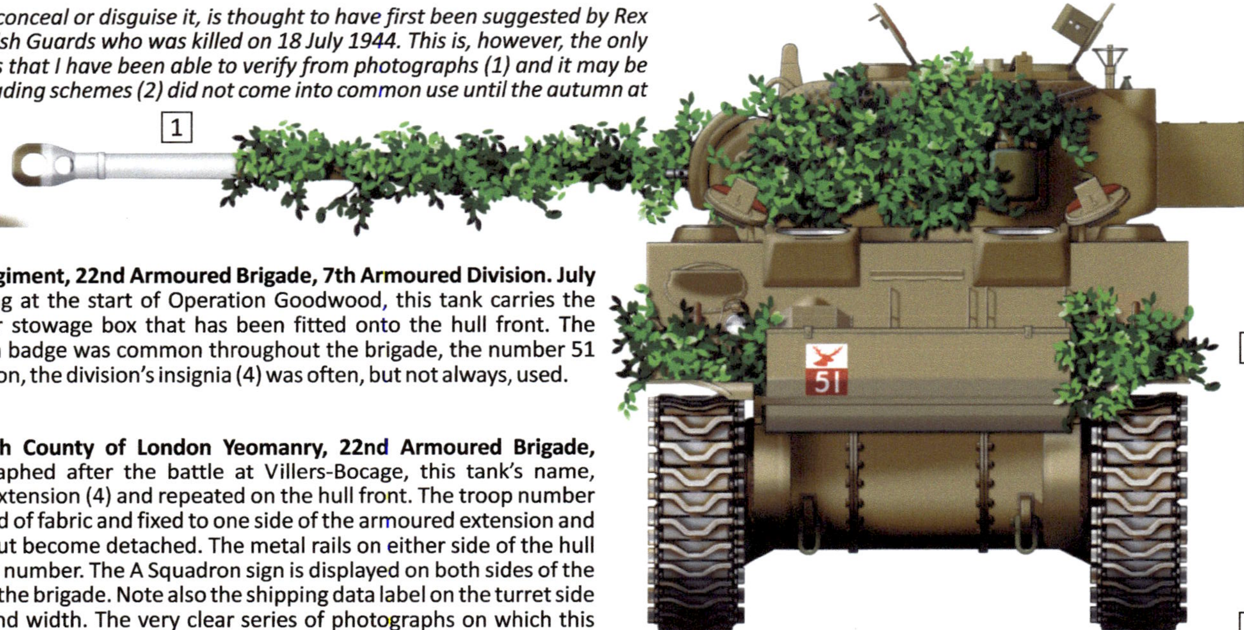

2

3

3

At right: Sherman VC Firefly. 1st Royal Tank Regiment, 22nd Armoured Brigade, 7th Armoured Division. July 1944. Photographed at the Orne River crossing at the start of Operation Goodwood, this tank carries the brigade's colourful formation badge on a rear stowage box that has been fitted onto the hull front. The combination of the AoS sign and the formation badge was common throughout the brigade, the number 51 here indicating the senior regiment (3). In addition, the division's insignia (4) was often, but not always, used.

Below: Sherman VC Firefly. A Squadron, 4th County of London Yeomanry, 22nd Armoured Brigade, 7th Armoured Division. June 1944. Photographed after the battle at Villers-Bocage, this tank's name, *Allakeefek*, is painted on the rear of the turret extension (4) and repeated on the hull front. The troop number (5) appears to have been painted onto some kind of fabric and fixed to one side of the armoured extension and it is probable that it was displayed elsewhere but become detached. The metal rails on either side of the hull obscure the anti-freeze warning (6) and the WD number. The A Squadron sign is displayed on both sides of the turret in blue, identifying the junior regiment of the brigade. Note also the shipping data label on the turret side showing the vehicle's weight, height, length and width. The very clear series of photographs on which this illustration was based confirm that no formation badge or AoS sign were carried. The name is an anglicised Arabic word meaning a lack of concern or consideration.

4

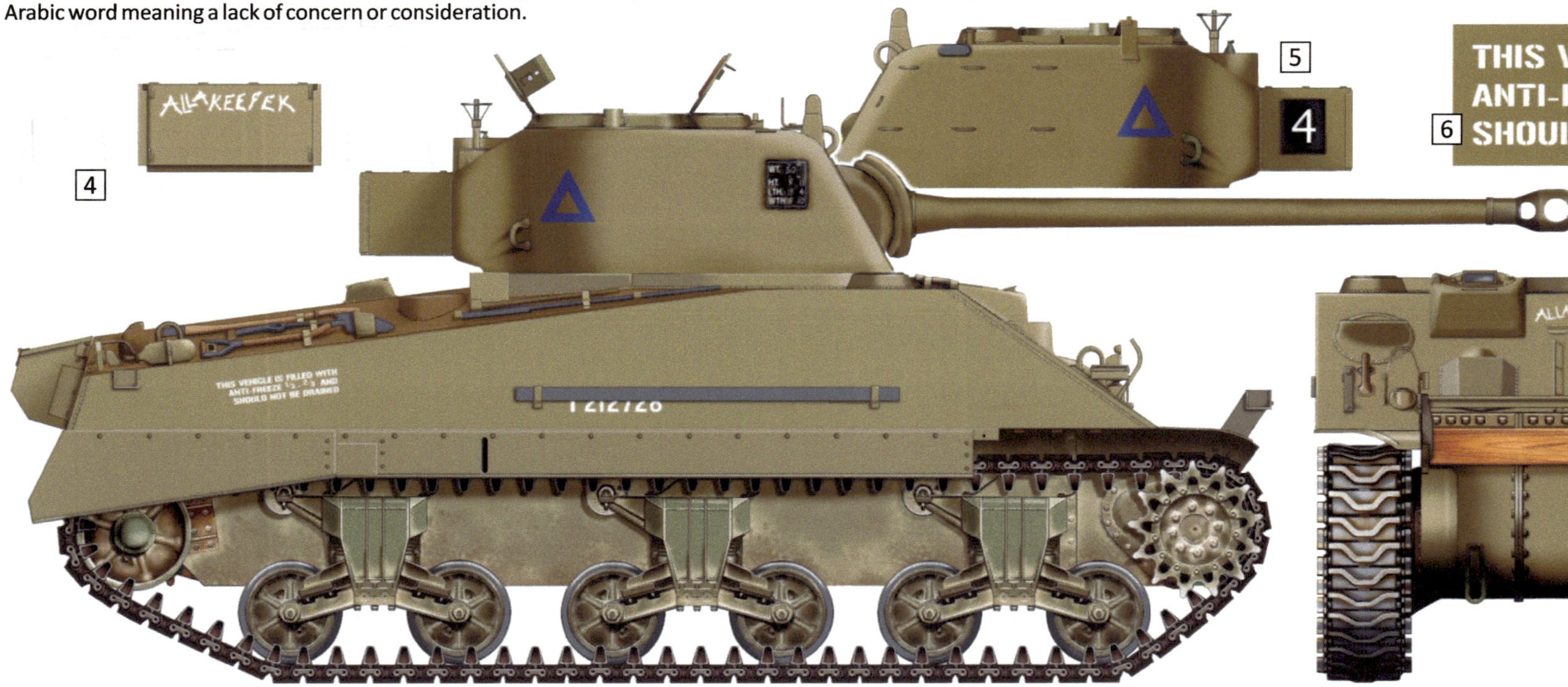

5

6

THIS VEHICLE IS FILLED WITH
ANTI-FREEZE $1/3$ - $2/3$ AND
SHOULD NOT BE DRAINED

At right: Sherman V OP. Headquarters, 29th Armoured Brigade, 11th Armoured Division. June 1944. The personal mount of Brigadier 'Roscoe' Harvey, the commander of 29th Armoured Brigade, this tank has the early direct vision blocks in front of the driver's and lap gunner's hoods. These were dropped from production in August 1942 and those seen here have been welded shut, as most were by this time. The AoS sign of 50 on a red square identifies the headquarters of an armoured brigade and the division's formation badge (1) has also been applied to the differential housing. The name *'Kay'*, rendered by an obviously accomplished hand, probably refers to the driver's wife or sweetheart (2). Note the ammunition box welded to the left side fender and marked *Command Tank*, probably in white. Photographs of this tank can be seen on page 13 and page 15.

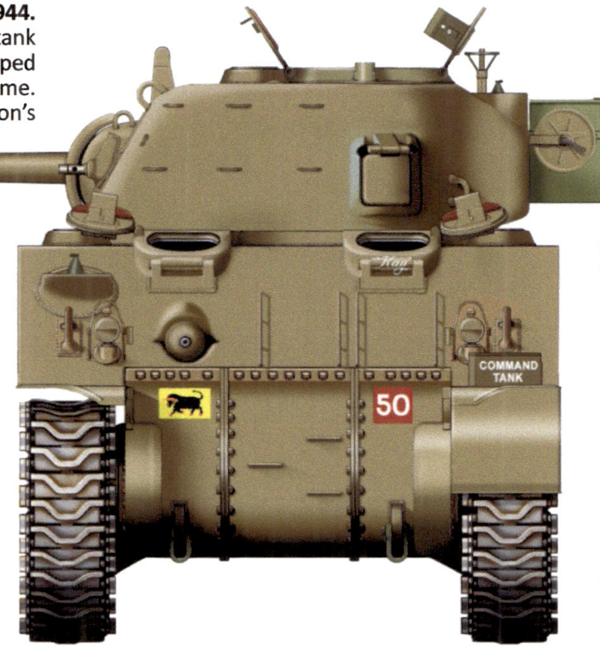

1

2

Above: A large box, fixed to the turret side, was commonly seen on tanks of this regiment.

Below: Sherman V OP. Headquarters Squadron, 23rd Hussars, 29th Armoured Brigade, 11th Armoured Division. July 1944. As with most OP tanks, an aerial fitting has been attached to the antenna bracket (3) and, as can be seen from our photograph, there appears to be an additional aerial on the vehicle's left-hand side, visible here behind the blanket box. With the bracket welded to the turret side, just above the lifting ring, this makes five attachments for wireless aerials in total. The diamond-shaped company sign denotes the regimental headquarters, depicted here in the red colour of the brigade's senior regiment.

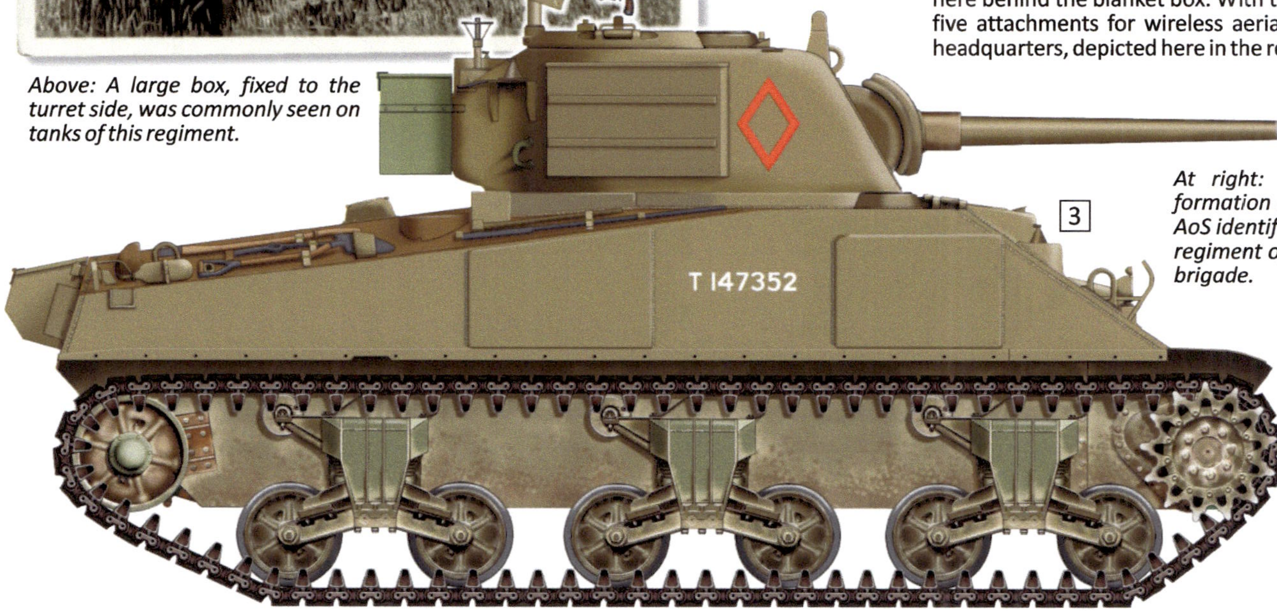

3

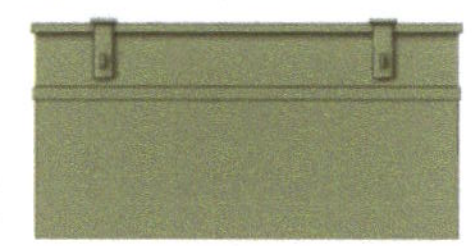

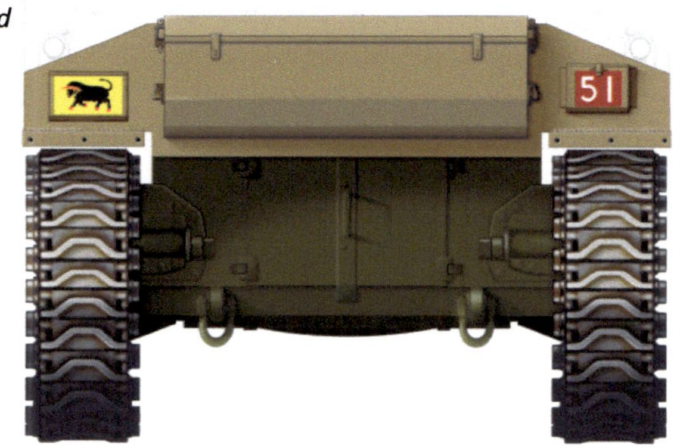

At right: The division's formation badge and the AoS identifying the senior regiment of an armoured brigade.

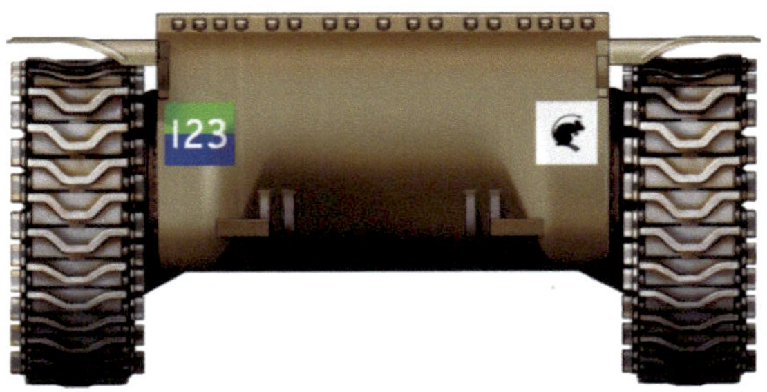

At left: The formation badge of 4th Armoured Brigade, a variation of the famous Desert Rat insignia.

Above: The very unusual AoS sign adopted by this brigade some time after the amalgamation of the two Yeomanry regiments. That the square is made up of two colours is apparent from our photographs and the late William Platz, an authority with whom I am reluctant to disagree, stated emphatically that the colours were green over blue.

Above and above, left: Sherman II. B Squadron, 3rd/4th County of London Yeomanry, 4th Armoured Brigade. August 1944. Photographed shortly after the Normandy battles, this Sherman II is typical of the regiment's tanks at that time. The WD number is rendered in US Army Blue Drab, suggesting that these tanks were not repainted and the B Squadron square on the turret encloses the troop number. All the regiment's tanks were numbered, perhaps sequentially throughout the regiment or with blocks of letters allocated to each company as they were during this regiment's service in Italy, although the numbers used were definitely not the same.

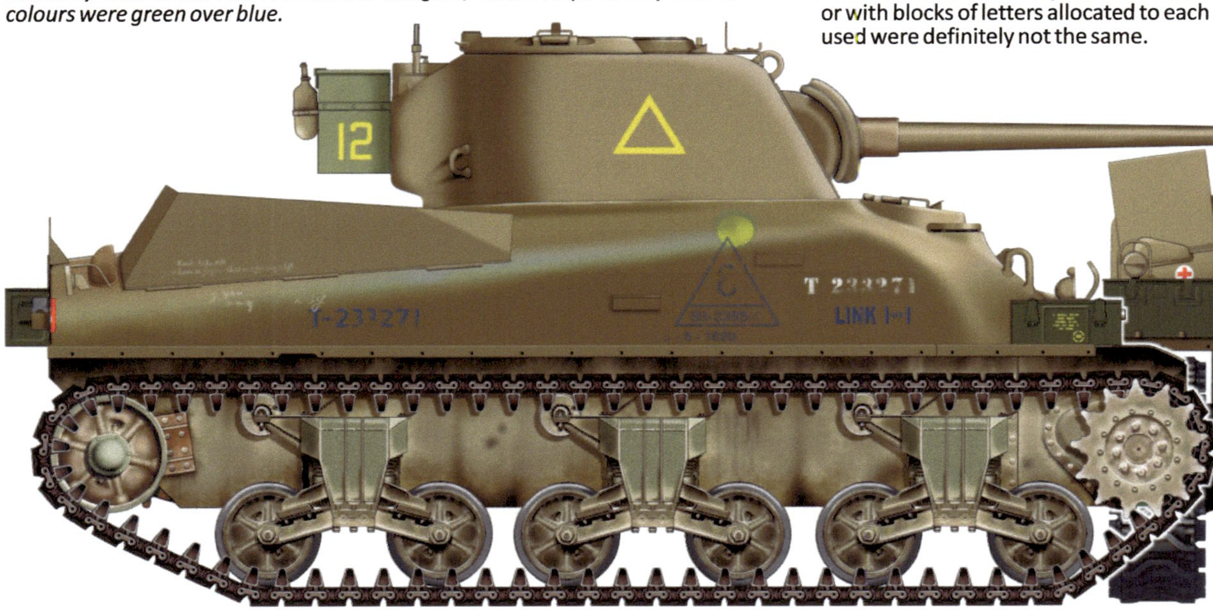

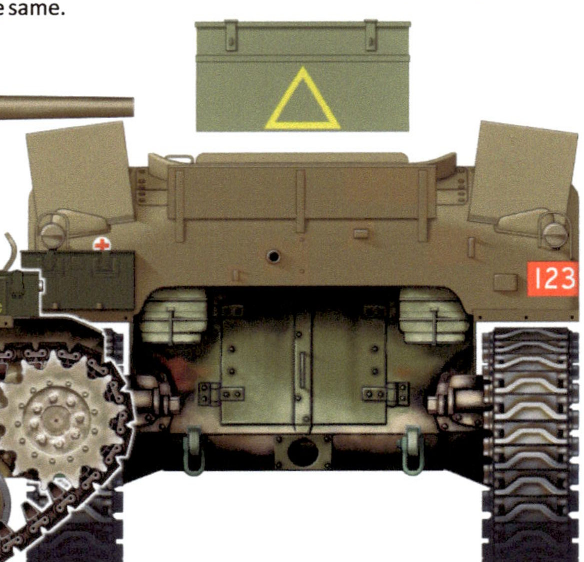

Sherman II. A Squadron, 3rd County of London Yeomanry, 4th Armoured Brigade. July 1944. The sections of sandshield, fitted to the hull sides as additional stowage space, was a common feature of this brigade's tanks. Note that this vehicle still carries the shipping markings applied in the United States. The brigade's formation badge on the rear hull is obscured by the large box welded to the rear plate. The yellowish circle on the hull side is poison gas detection paint.

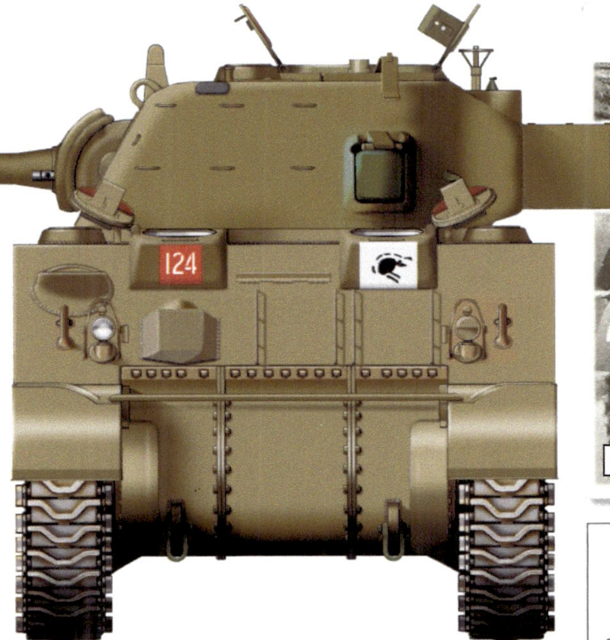

Sherman VC Firefly. 44th Royal Tank Regiment, 4th Armoured Brigade. June 1944. As with most tanks of this brigade, this Firefly has sections of sandshield welded to the hull sides to allow the crew to carry additional stores or equipment (7). The turret has no markings, unlike the tank depicted below which carries a sign identifying A Squadron in blue, denoting the junior regiment of an armoured brigade, with troop number in white. Compare the very rudimentary formation badge, obviously executed with a stencil, to that shown on page 20. Interestingly the photograph at right shows the two-colour AoS sign and although this version seems to have the colours reversed, the difference is probably due to the type of film stock used.

6

1 2 3 4 5

At left: 1. A variation of the brigade's formation badge also show in the photograph (6) above. The system of Arm of Service signs used by 4th Armoured Brigade: 2. Brigade headquarters. 3. The Royal Scots Greys. 4. 3rd County of London Yeomanry amalgamated with 4th County of London Yeomanry from 29 July 1944. 5. 44th Royal Tank Regiment

7

Right: Sherman II. 44th Royal Tank Regiment, 4th Armoured Brigade. June 1944. In addition to the sections of sandshield welded to the hull sides, this tank also has two field-modified stowage bins fixed to the rear plate. The lower half of the wading stack is still in place as many were throughout the Normandy campaign. The tanks of this regiment were named, beginning with the letter R in keeping with RTR tradition.

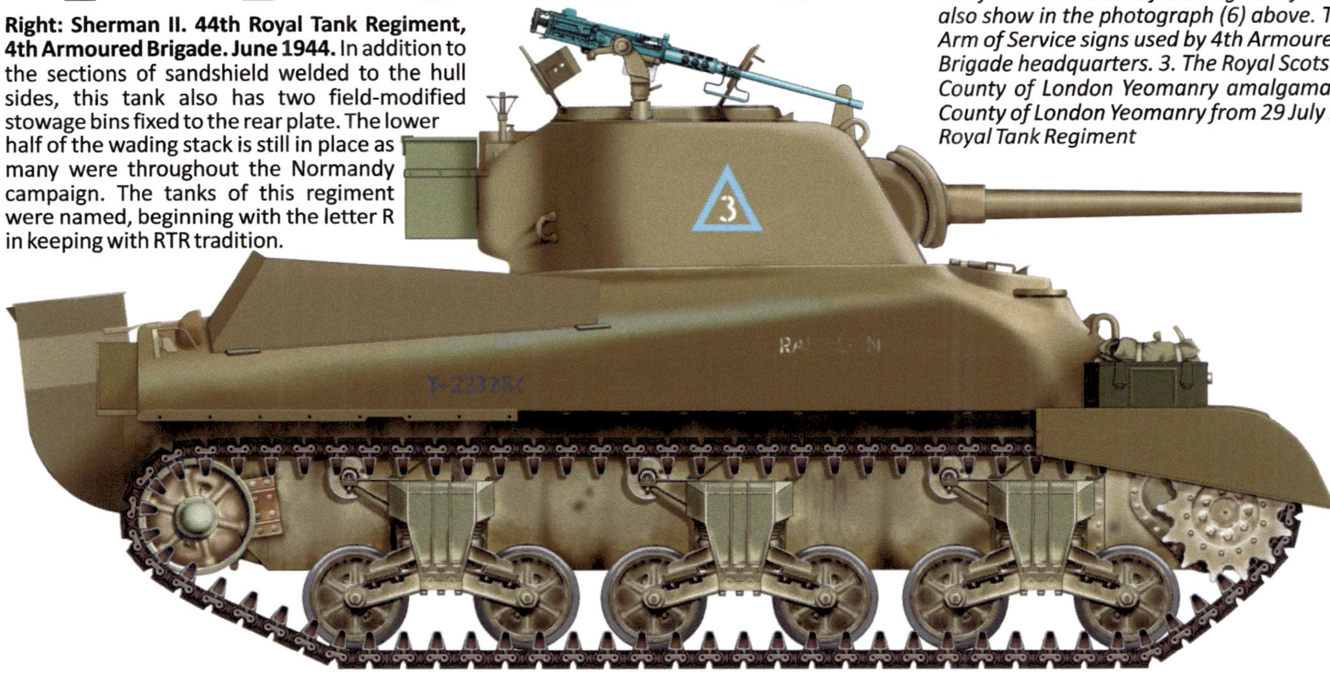

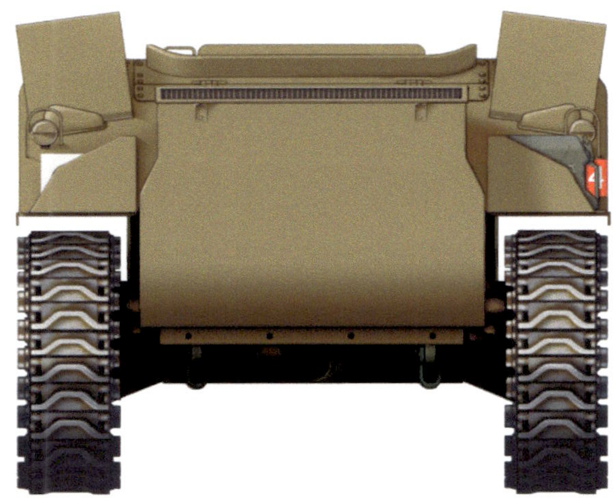

At right: Sherman IC Hybrid Firefly. 3rd Royal Tank Regiment, 29th Armoured Brigade, 11th Armoured Division. July 1944. Photographed near Aunay-sur-Odon on 31 July 1944, the identification with 3rd RTR is largely based on the location and uniform details of the commander, both of which are apparent in the photograph on which this illustration is based. As a means of camouflage, strips of khaki-coloured hessian were secured to the tank by lengths of rope, nets or even chicken wire. Note that the rear hull stowage box has been moved to the hull front, a practice which became more common as the fighting in Normandy went on. The mixed style of lettering used to render the WD number is often seen on IC Fireflies.

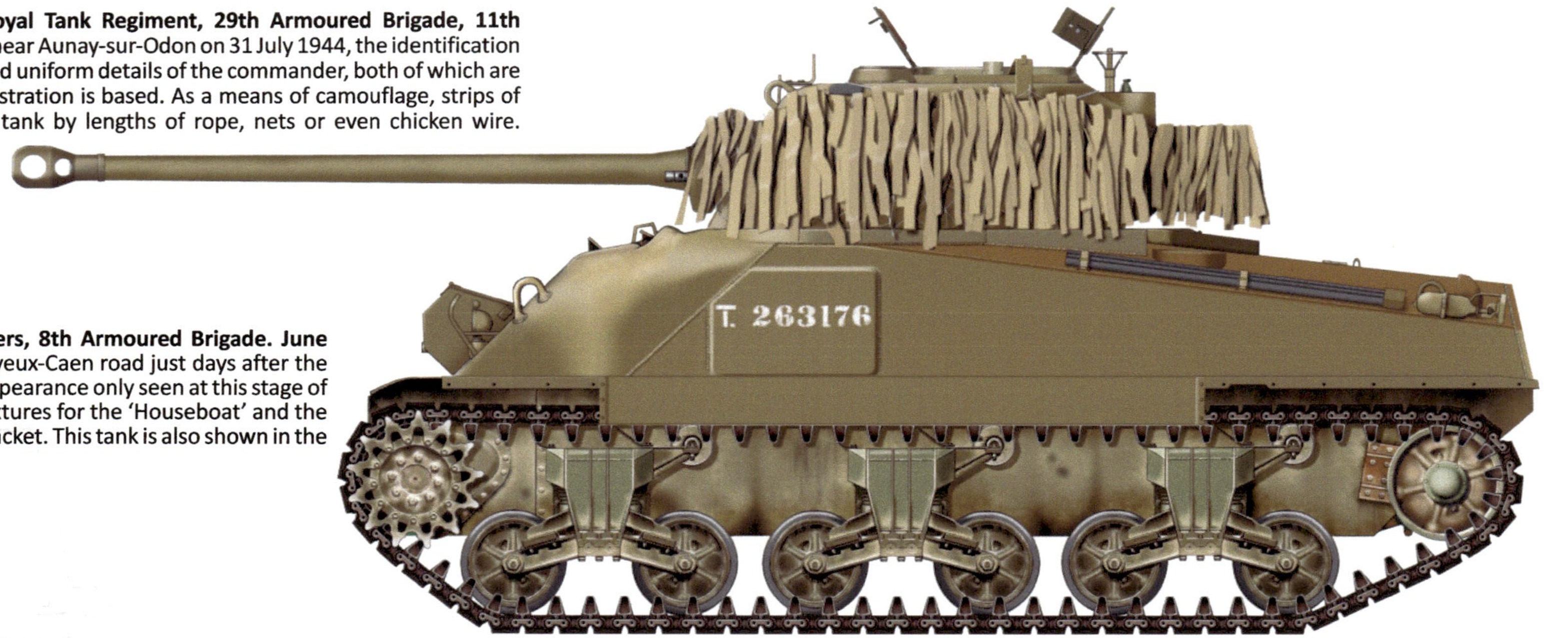

Sherman VC Firefly. A Squadron, 24th Lancers, 8th Armoured Brigade. June 1944. Photographed near St. Léger on the Bayeux-Caen road just days after the invasion, this tank exhibits the neat and tidy appearance only seen at this stage of the operation. Of note are the brackets and fixtures for the 'Houseboat' and the large, non-standard cover over the antenna bracket. This tank is also shown in the photograph at the bottom of page 51.

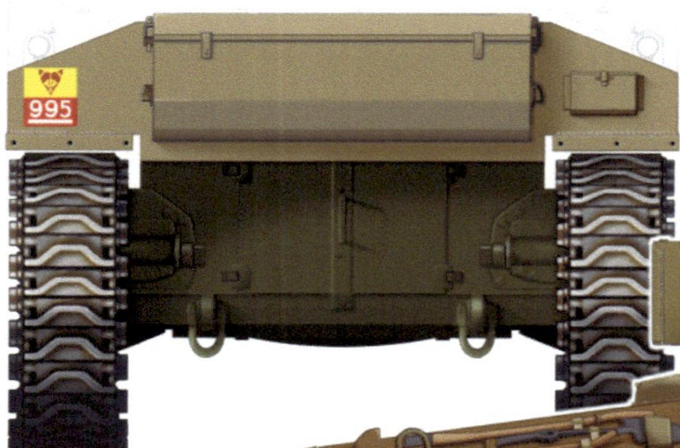

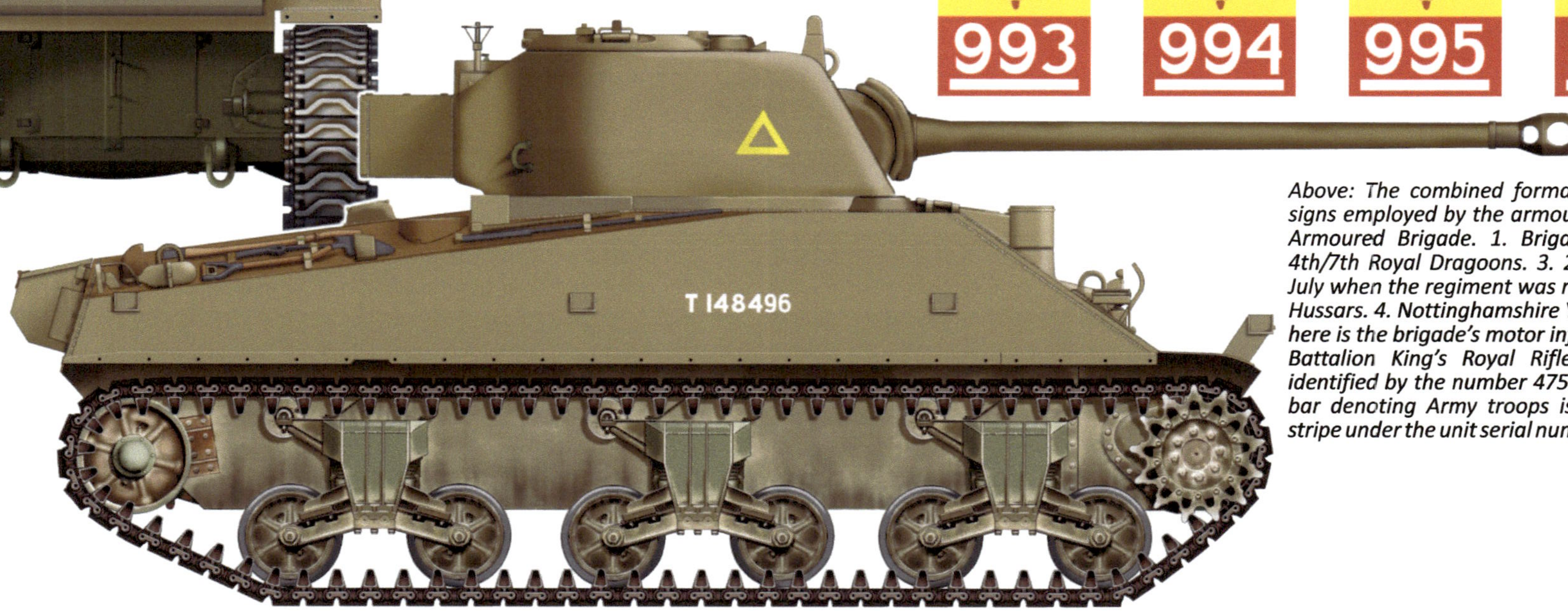

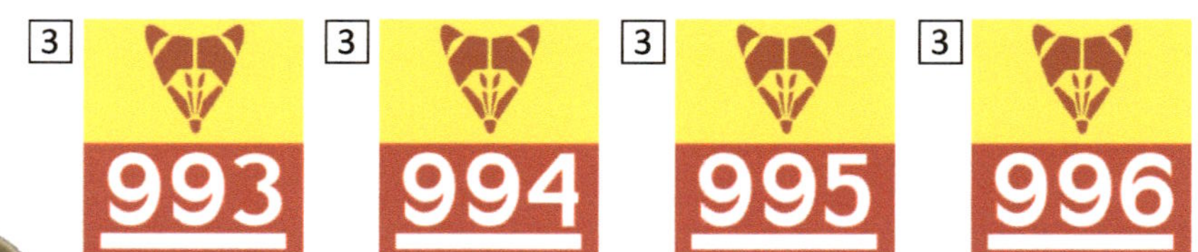

Above: The combined formation badge and AoS signs employed by the armoured regiments of 8th Armoured Brigade. 1. Brigade headquarters. 2. 4th/7th Royal Dragoons. 3. 24th Lancers until 29 July when the regiment was replaced by 13th/18th Hussars. 4. Nottinghamshire Yeomanry. Not shown here is the brigade's motor infantry battalion, 12th Battalion King's Royal Rifle Corps, which was identified by the number 475. Note that the white bar denoting Army troops is rendered as a thin stripe under the unit serial number.

At right: Sherman III. Headquarters, 13th/18th Royal Hussars, 27th Armoured Brigade. June 1944. The tanks of this regiment all carried large red numbers, outlined in white, on the turret sides and rear of the blanket box (1) as shown here. The tanks of A squadron were numbered from 22-36, with B Squadron using 44-58, C Squadron from 60-80 while the headquarters tanks used numbers below 20. The tanks were all named, the names beginning with the squadron letter, with the exception of the headquarters which seem to have chosen the names at random (2). The names were displayed on a black panel on the hull side (3). Of note are the brackets fitted to the rear hull, the cable reel attached to the blanket box, the strut for the smoke dischargers on the turret side and the lower half of the wading stack which is still in place. Photographs of this tank appear on page 3 and page 53.

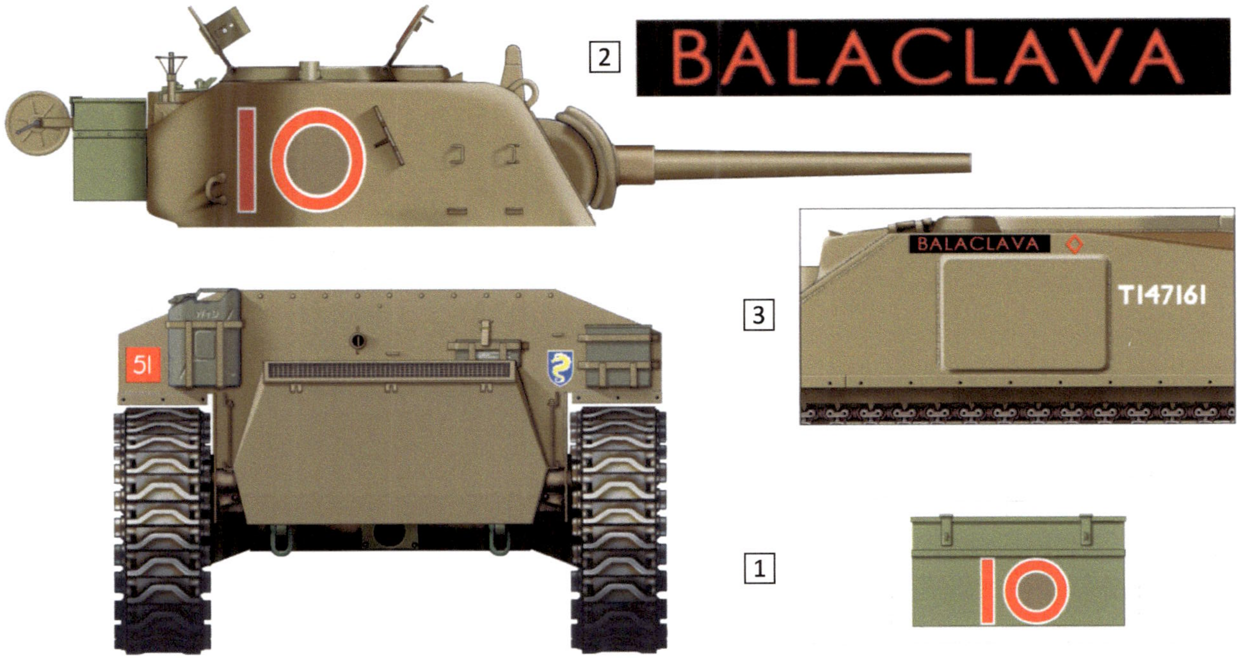

Sherman VC Firefly. A Squadron, East Riding Yeomanry, 27th Armoured Brigade. June 1944. The tanks of this regiment also carried large numbers on the turret sides and on the blanket box (4). Their exact significance is not fully understood at this time and it may be that the tanks were simply numbered consecutively throughout the regiment. In recent years it has been suggested that the call sign numbers may have been rendered in the colours denoting the regiment's seniority within the brigade and a study of the available photographs would seem to confirm this. On the very clear photograph on which this illustration is based, it is possible to discern the troop number at the centre of the squadron sign and a faint white drop shadow on the name *Spitfire* (5). Note the bracket on the turret towards the front used for holding spare track links. Most, if not all, the tanks of 27th Armoured Brigade were fitted with these just prior to the invasion. A photograph of this tank can be seen on page 53.

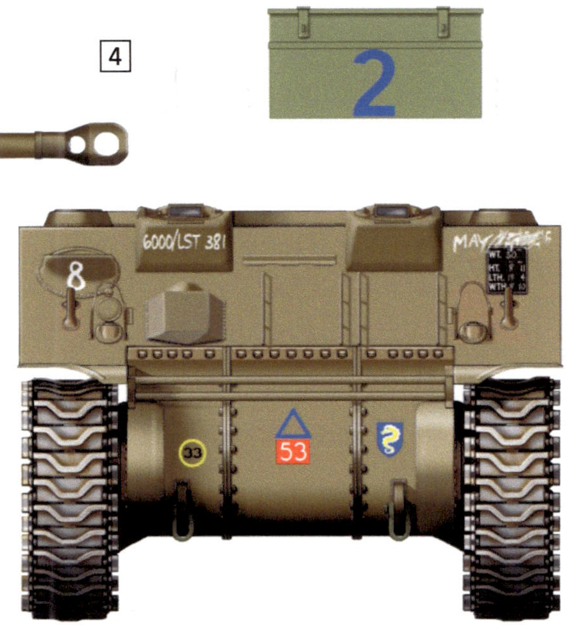

1

2

3 4 5 6

At left: The system of AoS signs used by 27th Armoured Brigade. 3. Brigade headquarters. 4. 13th/18th Hussars. 5. The East Riding Yeomanry. 6. The Staffordshire Yeomanry. Unlike the other independent formations, this follows the numbering system employed by the brigades of the armoured divisions.

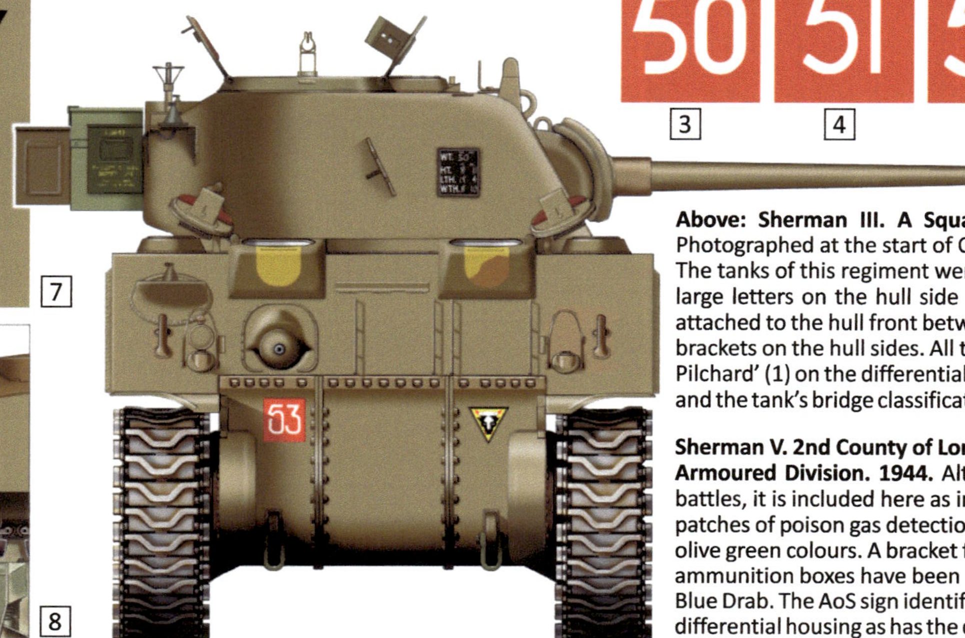

7

8

Above: Sherman III. A Squadron, Staffordshire Yeomanry, 27th Armoured Brigade. July 1944. Photographed at the start of Operation Goodwood, this may be the tank of the squadron commander. The tanks of this regiment were all named using the squadron letter system with the names painted in large letters on the hull side as shown here. Most tanks of this brigade had the metal bars or rods attached to the hull front between the fenders as a means of holding spare track links in addition to the brackets on the hull sides. All tanks carried the formation badge, known affectionately as the 'Pregnant Pilchard' (1) on the differential housing. Also shown are the A Squadron symbol, the regiment's AoS sign and the tank's bridge classification (2).

Sherman V. 2nd County of London Yeomanry (Westminster Dragoons), 30th Armoured Brigade, 79th Armoured Division. 1944. Although this tank was photographed at some time after the Normandy battles, it is included here as images of this division's Sherman OP tanks are quite rare. Of note are the patches of poison gas detection paint on the hoods in what appears to be the both early khaki and later olive green colours. A bracket for an additional wireless antenna has been welded to the turret side and ammunition boxes have been attached to the blanket box. The tank's WD number (7) is rendered in US Blue Drab. The AoS sign identifying the second senior regiment of the brigade has been painted onto the differential housing as has the division's formation badge (8).

1 2 3 4

Above: *The AoS signs of 33rd Armoured Brigade. 1. Brigade headquarters. 2. 1st Northamptonshire Yeomanry. There is some evidence that this regiment's marking incorporated the white bar denoting Army level troops which the others, contrary to official guidelines, did not. 3. 144th RAC. 4. 148th RAC.*

At right: Sherman VC. A Squadron, 144th Royal Armoured Corps, 33rd Armoured Brigade. July 1944. Photographed at the start of Operation Charnwood, this vehicle is typical of the regiment's Fireflies and 75mm tanks. All were marked in a style very similar to the Shermans of 27th Armoured Brigade shown on pages 23 and 24. The regimental headquarters tanks were numbered from 12-17, those of A Squadron used 30-49, B Squadron 50-69 and C Squadron tanks were identified by numbers from 70-89. Most tanks had the AoS sign painted onto the first aid box on the rear hull plate and the brigade's Diabolo formation badge on the opposite side. The large wooden ammunition crates, sometimes painted, fixed to the hull deck in a purpose-built bracket were common, if not universal. The piece of equipment on the engine access doors is a smoke emitter.

5

This regiment was raised by converting 8th Battalion The East Lancashire Regiment to an armoured role and was one of the new RAC units that retained its original cap badge (5).

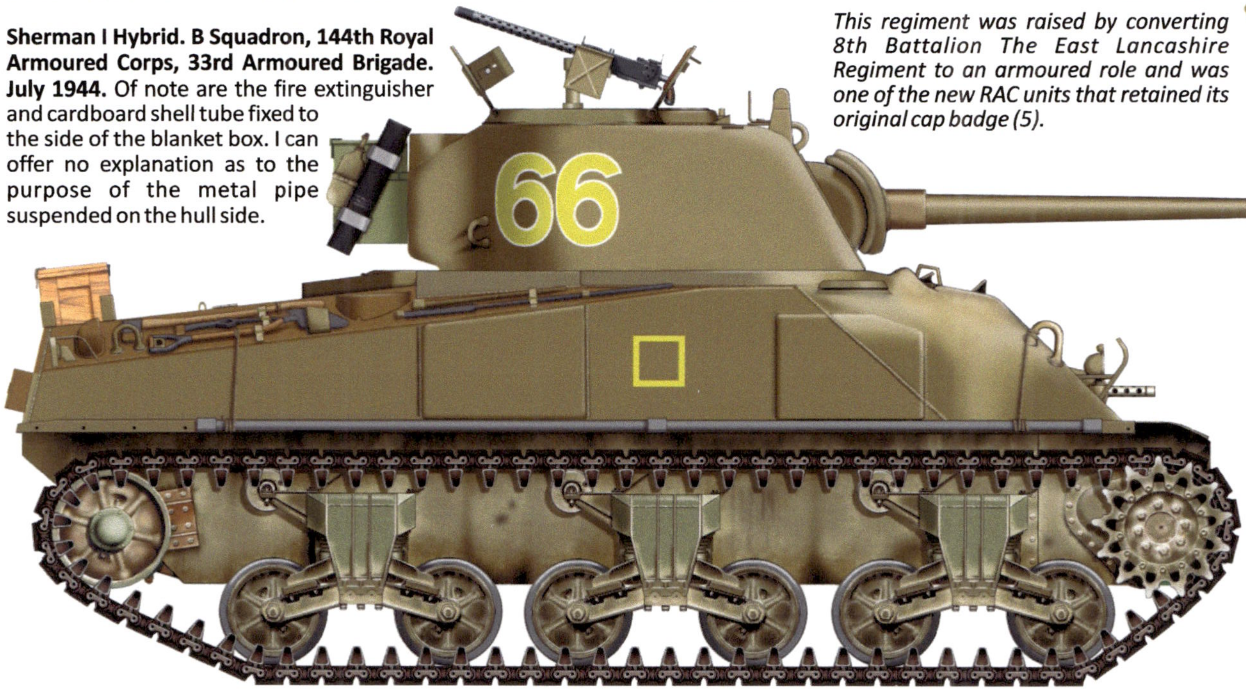

Sherman I Hybrid. B Squadron, 144th Royal Armoured Corps, 33rd Armoured Brigade. July 1944. Of note are the fire extinguisher and cardboard shell tube fixed to the side of the blanket box. I can offer no explanation as to the purpose of the metal pipe suspended on the hull side.

At left: An examination of the available photographs shows that the numbers on the blanket box were often applied without the outline. Note also that here the 75mm ammunition crate has not been painted.

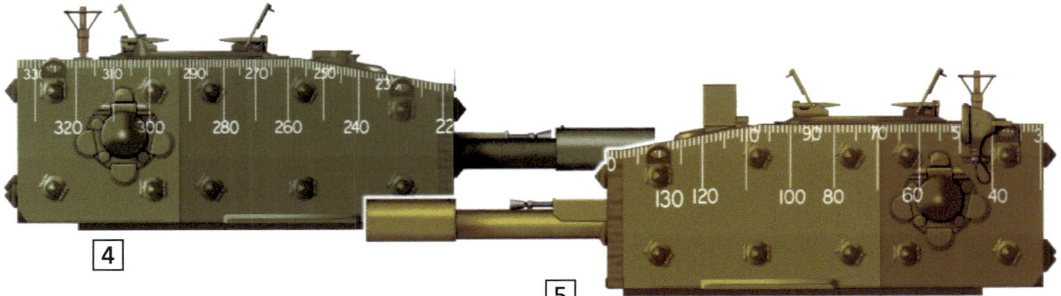

Below and right: Sherman V. 2nd Battery, Royal Marine Armoured Support Group. June 1944. Like most, but apparently not all, the tanks allocated to the Royal Marine Support Group for the D-Day landings, this vehicle has the distinctive compass rose painted in white numbers and gradations around the turret. In theory a crew member standing outside the turret could direct the tank's fire by lining up the numbers with the target. Note that the calibrations continue across the gun mount. The box in front of the commander's hatch is probably a cover for the No.12 Dial Sight with which all the tanks were fitted. In addition the Shermans of the Positioning Officers (PO) had a binnacle compass fitted to the turret interior. The name *Fox* indicates F Battery, as explained on pages 57 and 58. A red/white/red RAC recognition marking is painted at the centre of the differential housing and the AoS sign identifying 2nd Battery can be seen just to the right of the driver's position. Also shown is the aerial recognition sign authorised in April 1944 (1), the tank's bridge classification marking (2) and the standard shipping data label (3). In common with the Centaurs, the headlight brush guards of the Shermans were painted white. For the sake of completeness I have included left and right-hand side views of the Royal Marines Centaur tanks, one painted in SCC15 (4) and the other in SCC2 (5), both of which are possible.

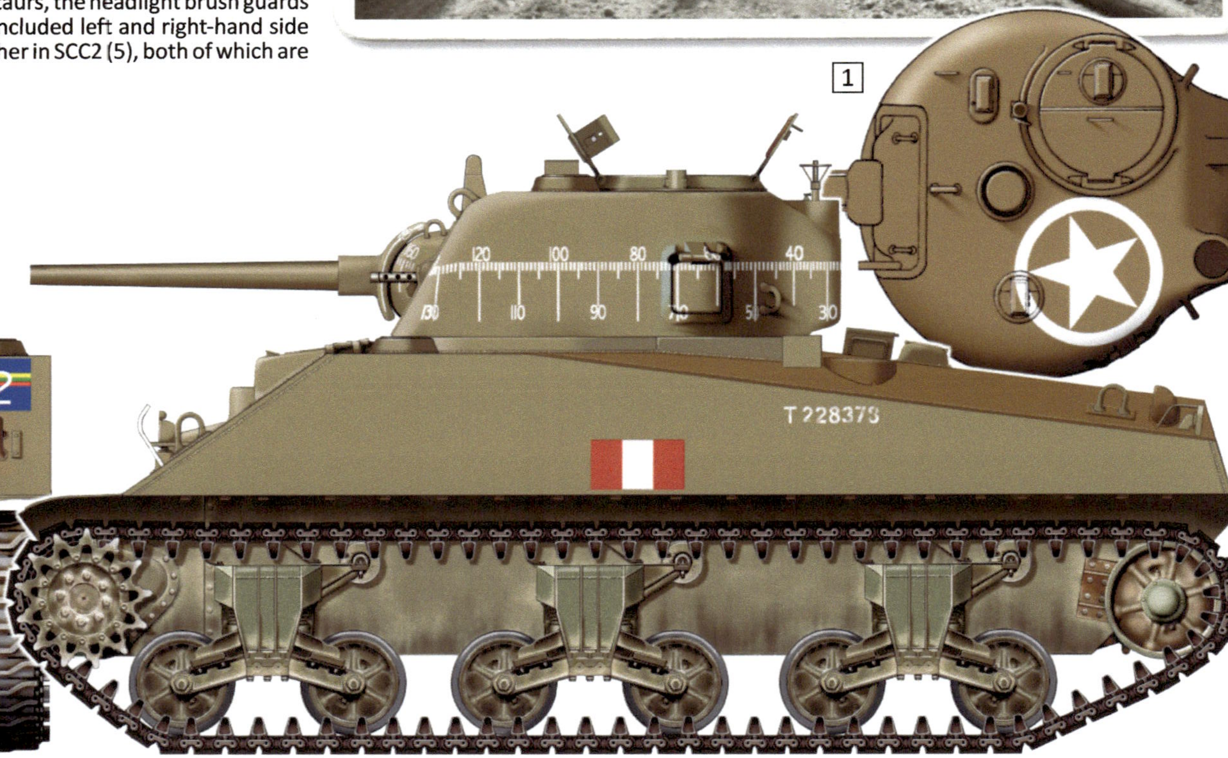

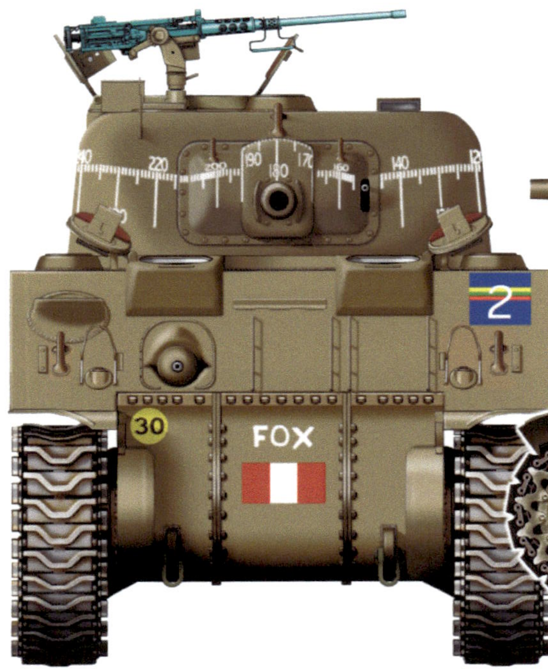

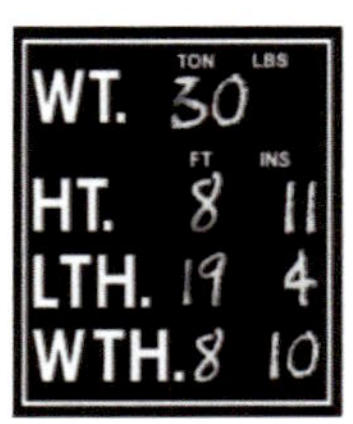

A

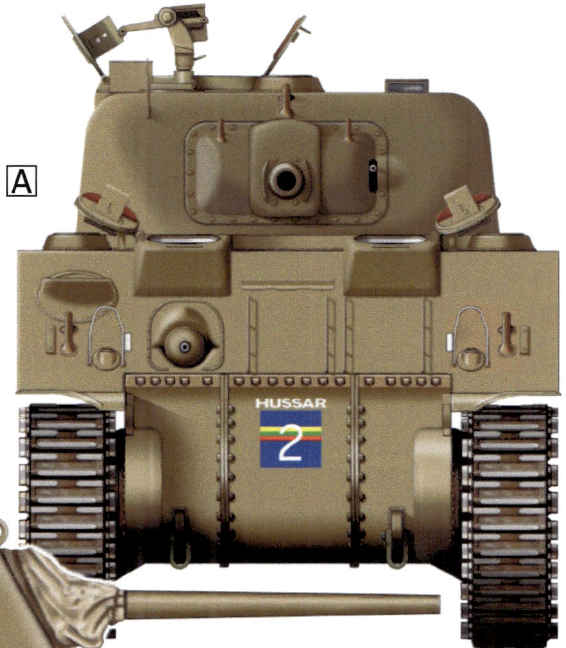

B

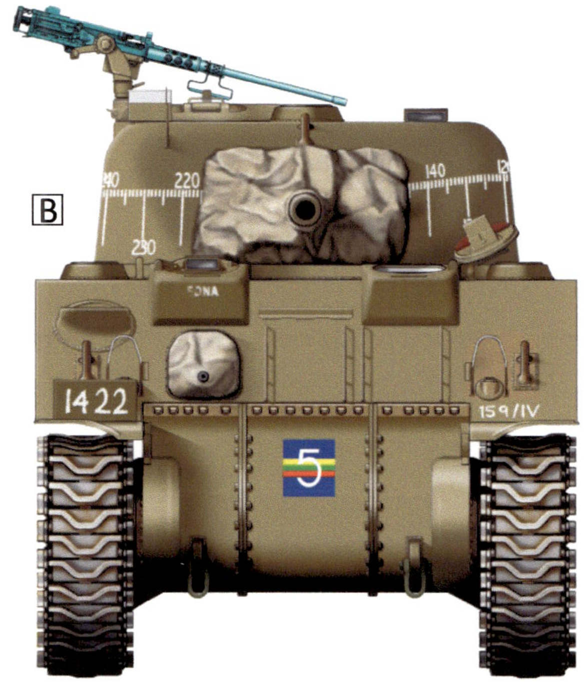

A. Sherman V. 2nd Battery, Royal Marine Armoured Support Group. 1944. Photographed at a collection point for damaged vehicles some time after the Normandy battles, this tank is unusual in that it appears not to have the compass rose applied to other Royal Marine tanks. It seems unlikely that it would have been removed and although the tank is damaged some trace would surely have remained, particularly as the other markings are in reasonably good condition. The name *Hussar* indicates H Troop of 2nd Battery. The large recognition marking on the hull side, complete with circle, is unusual. It seems that most of the Marines' Sherman tanks were fitted with the early M34 gun mantlet.

B. Sherman V. 5th Battery, Royal Marine Armoured Support Group. June 1944. Filmed on Queen Sector, Sword Beach early on the morning of 6 June 1944, the identification with 5th Battery is largely based on the location which has been confirmed. The AoS sign on the differential housing is completely conjectural, this area being covered by a length of spare track in the film, but the remainder of the hull glacis is visible and the position here is at least possible. The name on the lap gunner's hood is indecipherable but may be *Edna*, a wife or girlfriend, and the chalked markings above each fender are loading numbers indicating the tank's place in the landing craft. Note the waterproofing on the main gun and the machine gun.

At left: The battery AoS signs, all based on actual examples, mostly Centaurs. Note that each is slightly different and that although the blue section appears quite light in monochrome photographs, the royal blue depicted here is correct.

A

B

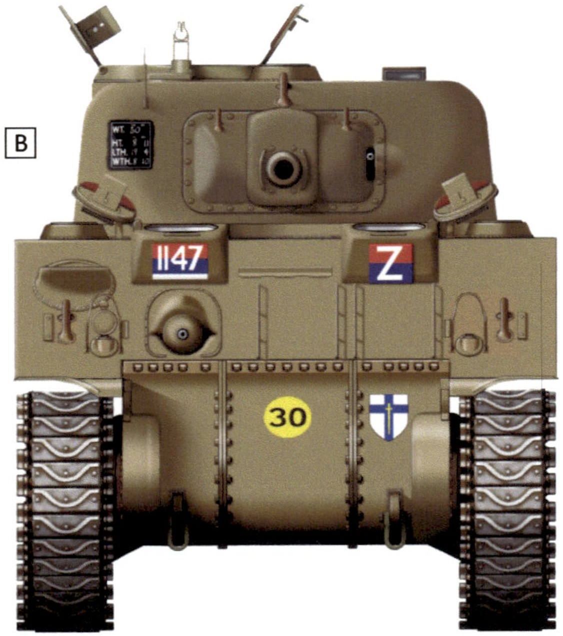

A. Sherman V AOP. 86th (East Anglia, Hertfordshire Yeomanry) Field Regiment, RA. June 1944. This regiment supported 50th (Northumbrian) Division during the landings and was later attached to 8th Armoured Brigade. The white bar at the bottom of the AoS sign identifies a regiment under direct Army command and the formation badge of 2nd Army can be seen on the differential housing. The artillery tactical sign combining the letters GD in white on a red over blue square identifies the gun position officer of 2nd Battery's D Troop.

B. Sherman V AOP. 86th (East Anglia, Hertfordshire Yeomanry) Field Regiment, RA. June 1944. Photographed in England immediately prior to the invasion, this tank displays slightly different markings to the other Sherman OP of the same regiment. The artillery tactical sign of a white letter Z on a red over blue square denotes the regimental commander, at that time Lieutenant Colonel G.D. Fanshawe, who was later promoted to command the artillery brigade of 3rd Infantry Division. Note that the tactical sign has been painted onto a panel and attached to the front of the driver's hood.

C. Sherman V AOP. 33rd Field Regiment, RA. June 1944. Photographed just inland from the invasion beaches near Hermanville-sur-Mer, this tank has field modified racks made from wooden boards supported by metal beams on each side of the hull. Note also the cable reel on the hull glacis, the .30 calibre machine gun and the aerial recognition marking on the turret, just visible here. It is unclear what other markings may have been applied to this tank but a photograph of a Priest self-propelled gun of the same unit has the division's formation badge painted onto the differential housing. Two jerry cans, one of British manufacture and the other American, have been strapped to the turret side.

Far left: The formation badge of 3rd Infantry Division. At left. The formation badge of 2nd Army. Many variations existed albeit with slight differences only.

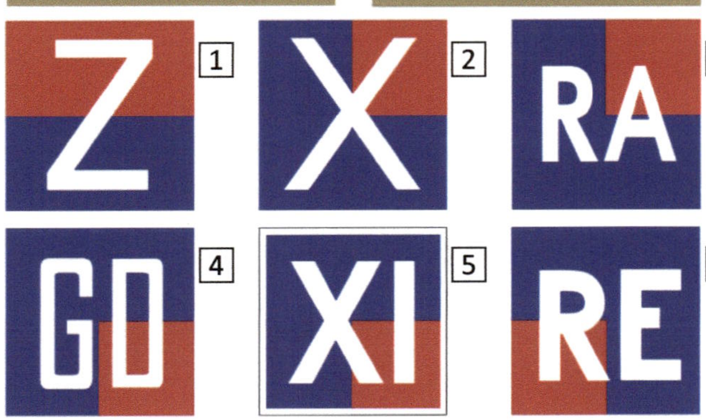

Far left: Examples of Royal Artillery Tactical signs. 1. Battery commander, 1st (P) Battery. 2. Battery commander, 2nd (Q) Battery. 3. An unofficial example seen on a Sherman AOP of 5th Royal Horse Artillery. 4. Troop commander, A Troop. the forward OP officer. 5. Second-in-command A Troop, the gun position officer. 6. Troop commander, E Troop.

C

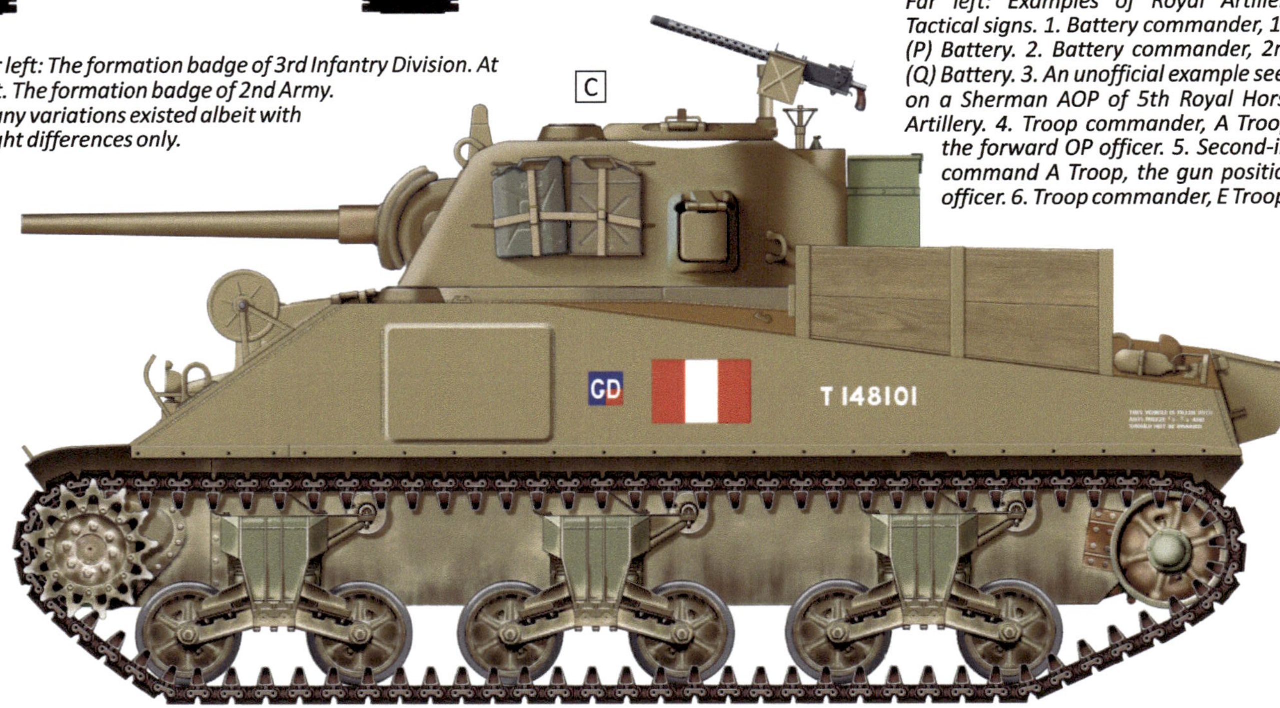

SHERMAN VC FIREFLY

1/35 Scale

JOHN THAM

John's model is based on the Tasca Firefly kit with many scratch-built details and hand-painted markings. As the campaign in North-west Europe progressed German hand-held anti-tank weapons, such as the Panzerfaust, were encountered more often and the addition of supplementary armour in the form of lengths of track were commonly seen. The figures were assembled and painted by Singaporean modeller Edmund Tan.

SHERMAN V

2nd Battery, Royal Marine Armoured Support Group

1/35 Scale

MARCOS SERRA

Marcos' model was built using the Dragon M4A4 kit with markings from Bison Decals, which this author helped design some years ago. Small parts, such as the tools, were included with the kit or were scratch built. The Centaur was built at the same time and both models were finished with Tamiya acrylics. These tanks are also shown and discussed on pages 26 and 27.

Based on the Resicast Sherman II kit, Shin Oikawa's build features extensive detailing. Note the periscope on the open hatch of the commander's cupola and on the hull roof in front of the vane sight.

SHERMAN II

44th Battalion, Royal Tank Regiment, 4th Armoured Brigade

1/35 Scale

SHIN OIKAWA

Sharp-eyed readers will have noticed that the squadron marking should be blue to denote the junior regiment of the brigade. This small error does not, however, detract from the overall effect of the model which captures the blunt, rough look of the cast hull and turret.

Incorporating many scratch-built features, this model includes parts from kits by Verlinden Productions, AFV Club, Asuka Model, Tamiya and Bronco. As there were no commercially available transfers, Shin made his own to depict a Firefly of the Sharpshooters. This tank was disabled and subsequently captured by the Germans after the battle at Villers-Bocage on 13 June 1944. Another tank of A Squadron, lost in the same engagement, is depicted on page 18.

SHERMAN VC FIREFLY

3rd County of London Yeomanry, 22nd Armoured Brigade, 7th Armoured Division

1/35 Scale

SHIN OIKAWA

SHERMAN V CRAB

1st Lothians and Border Horse, 30th Armoured Brigade, 79th Armoured Division

1/35 Scale

ANTONIO MARTIN TELLO

Antonio's highly detailed model is based on the hull from the Dragon Models M4A4 mated to the Tamiya M4 turret with the Resicast conversion set.

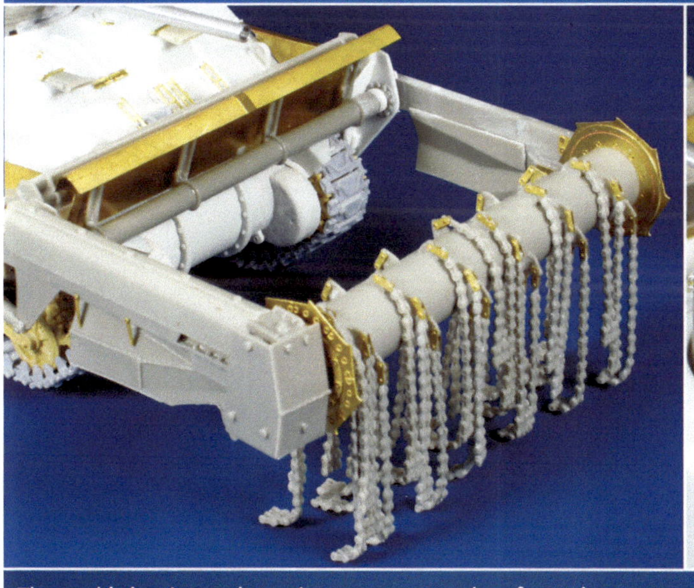

The tank's bogies and running gear were taken from the Academy Sherman kit with RHPS tracks, now marketed by Panda Plastics, a Jordi Rubio metal barrel and various Aber PE parts. The tools are made by Verlinden Productions and the .50 calibre machine gun is from Custom Dioramics

The model was finished with Tamiya acrylics and oils with Vallejo acrylics and MIG Production pigments used for the weathering.

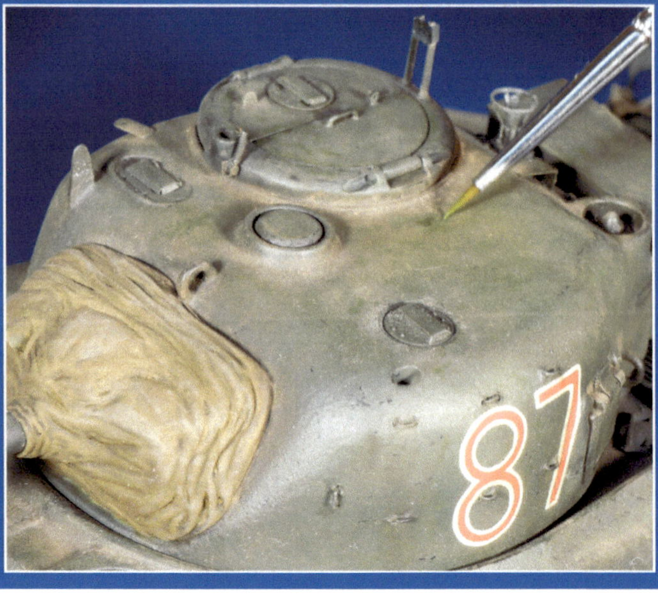

BEACH ARMOURED RECOVERY VEHICLE (BARV)

Royal Electrical and Mechanical Engineers

1/35 Scale

SHENG HUI

Built by the brains behind ROCHM Model, this replica features the company's own detailed conversion set which will soon be available for both the Dragon and Tasca kits. Just fifty-two of these vehicles were built by the time of the D-Day landings and all were based on the Sherman III. Operated by the five beach recovery sections of the Royal Mechanical and Electrical Engineers (REME) they were extremely successful in keeping the beaches clear.

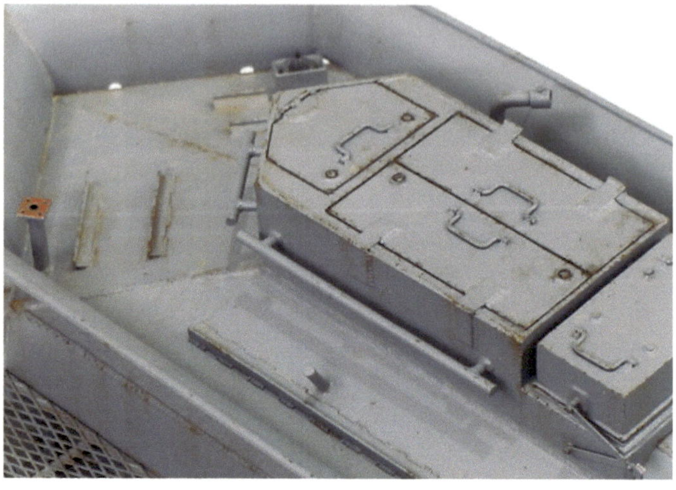

Although the M4 Medium Tank, which the British christened the Sherman, was one of the most important tanks of the latter half of the 20th century, with over 55,000 vehicles produced, it has only been little more than a decade since major model companies began releasing detailed versions. Prior to that, the few kits that were on the market were either re-releases of very old models, which required a great deal of work to produce an accurate replica, or short production run resin models. A number of small scale offerings were available from companies such as Fujimi, Hasegawa and the now defunct Italian company ESCI but most were, however, aimed at wargamers whose primary concern was not accuracy or detail but rather filling their armies with suitable tanks at a reasonable price in a short time. The venerable but extremely inaccurate Airfix Sherman fell into this category although, to be fair, it was first released in 1961. In contrast, the more recent models produced by companies like Tamiya, DML and Tasca are highly detailed replicas which increasingly feature photo-etched parts, detailed marking options and other after-market items as standard. The growth of interest in Allied armour by the major manufacturers has allowed the smaller, more specialised companies to flourish. Producing additional items in resin, photo-etched metal and other materials they offer a level of super-detailing which is only limited by the modeller's ability. As with the previous book in this series on the Tiger, I have chosen to concentrate on the most popular modelling scales of 1/35 and 1/48 although I have also included some of the smaller scale models. I should state that this list is far from exhaustive, mostly due to reasons of space and almost constant new releases, and I would encourage readers to undertake their own research into the areas that interest them most. An index of manufacturers can be found on page 64 of this book. In addition, the reader should be aware that I have included all versions which served with the British or Commonwealth armies although they may not be marketed as such. That is to say, they may lack some peculiarly British modifications such as the standard blanket box, tools or radio aerials but were nevertheless utilised in their basic form. Similarly I have omitted models or variants which were not taken up for service by the British military, such as the M4A3, or were not used during the Normandy campaign.

DRAGON MODELS LTD

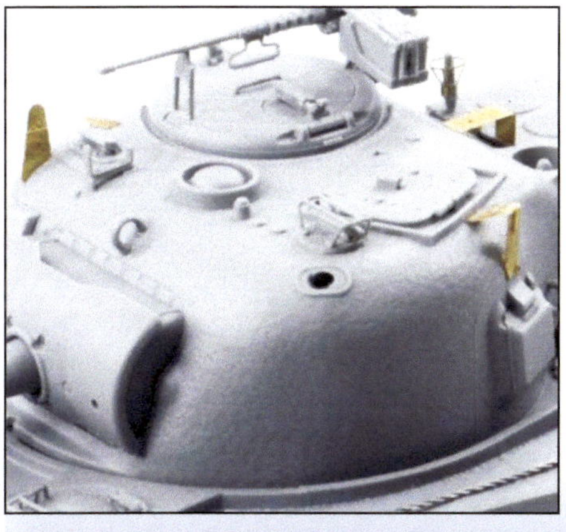

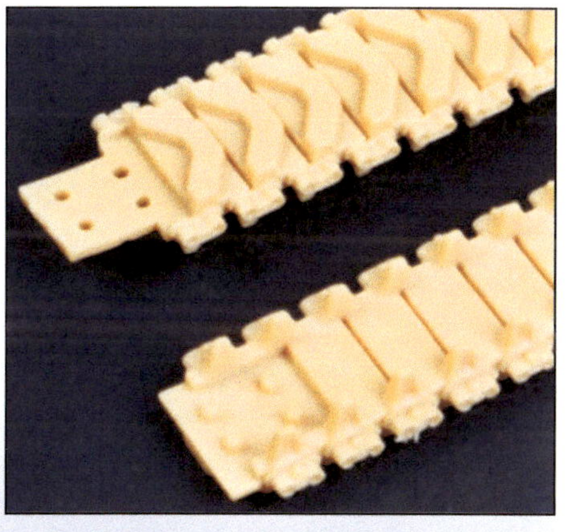

Above, from left to right: Dragon's 1/35 scale Firefly turret, a rear view of the 1/35 scale Firefly Ic hull and Dragon Models' so-called Magic Tracks depicting the T48 Rubber Chevron version. Below: Dragon's Sherman Mk III kit completed with the photo-etched set from Eduard Model Accessories. Although built as a tank that served in Sicily in 1943 this vehicle is essentially the same as those that fought in North-western Europe with the exception of the rails on the hull side and the MEF blanket box.

Above: M4A4 Sherman V in 1/72 scale and a part of the turret. Although this kit does contain distinctly British features, such as the Methyl Bromide fire extinguishers, there is no blanket box.

Based in Hong Kong, this company offers sixteen construction kits in both 1/35 and 1/72 scale and twelve assembled and pre-painted 1/72 scale display models. Dragon Models was one of the first of the major manufacturers to market accurate, highly detailed replicas of the Sherman and their small scale releases are some of the best on the market. Dragon's 1/35 scale kits that represent Sherman tanks in British service in North-west Europe include a Firefly VC, a Firefly VC with added .50 calibre machine gun and infantry figures and a Firefly IC Hybrid. The range of models of British army tanks serving on other fronts comprises three kits of the Sherman III with cast and direct vision hoods and an early Sherman II, all depicting tanks as they served in the Middle East or Italy. In addition to these there is an M4A4, an M4 with the composite hull and an M4 with welded hull. All these could, with some alteration, represent tanks serving with British regiments in Normandy. The section on technical details and modifications which begins on page 59 will explain this further. The 1/72 range of construction kits contains a Sherman V with 60lb Tulip rockets, although these were not used in Normandy, and a Sherman IC Firefly. In addition there are is an M4A1, an M4A4, an M4 with deep wading gear and a Sherman III. Of these only the latter can be build from the box as a British Army tank and would still need some alteration to represent the type seen in Normandy. In the pre-painted and assembled Armour series there are a number of models of the Firefly and Sherman III.

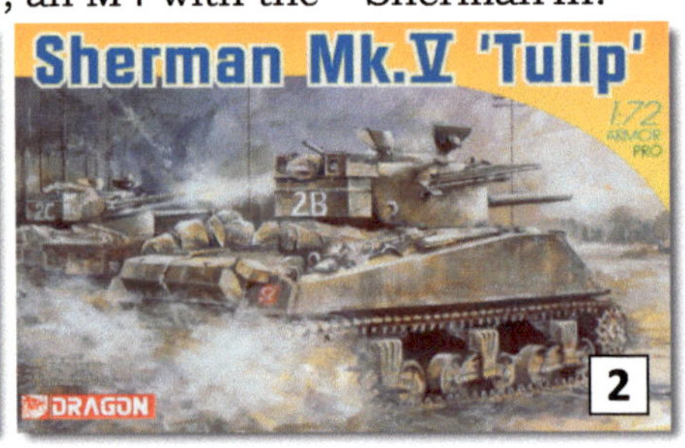

Above: 1. 1/35 scale Sherman III. With some exceptions, notably the mudguards and rails and the Mediterranean-style blanket box, these tanks are suitable for the Normandy period. 2. 1/72 scale Sherman V. The rockets were not used in Normandy. 3. 1/72 scale Firefly VC kit. 4. 1/35 scale Firefly IC Hybrid with additions from Eduard Model Accessories providing a good view of the ubiquitous blanket box. For some reason the armoured extension for the radio has been left off the turret bustle. 5. 1/35 scale Sherman VC Firefly kit built with upgrades from Royal Model.

TAMIYA INCORPORATED

Beginning life in the immediate post-war period as a sawmill and timber supply company, which also produced wooden ship and aeroplane models as a sideline, Tamiya Inc is today an international corporation. The company released a 1/21 scale Sherman M4 in 1963 and although a reasonable model for the time, it would be regarded as a toy today. Nevertheless, by the early 1970s Tamiya was producing a large range of armoured vehicles, figures and accessories and was almost solely responsible for the rise in popularity of 1/35 scale. For their day the kits were highly detailed and accurate but relatively easy to assemble and, importantly, affordable. The company's near monopoly of the market remained unchallenged until the release of the first Dragon Models kits in 1987. In 2003 Tamiya began releasing a series of models in 1/48 scale and this line has been extremely successful for the company, combining the potential for a high level of detail without the expense of the bigger kits. The 1/48 scale offerings include an early production version M4, an M4A1 and a Sherman IC Firefly. It should be noted that only the latter has all the fittings necessary to build a specifically British tank. At the time of writing Tamiya produces a US Army version of the M4 in 1/35 scale and a motorised M4A3, although this was never used operationally by the British Army. In 2014 Tamiya released a Firefly VC as a limited edition kit which was in fact the old Tasca model.

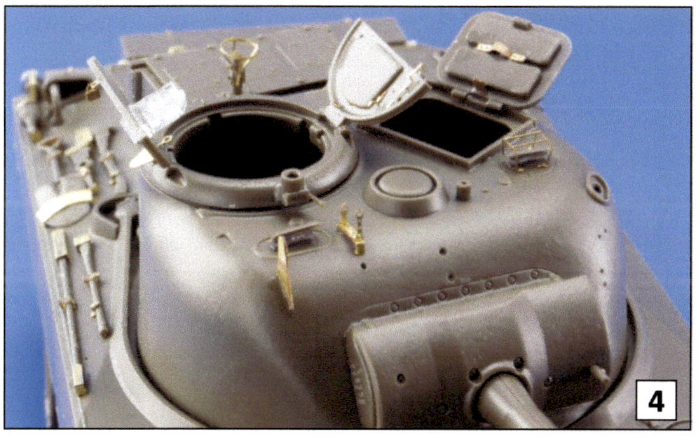

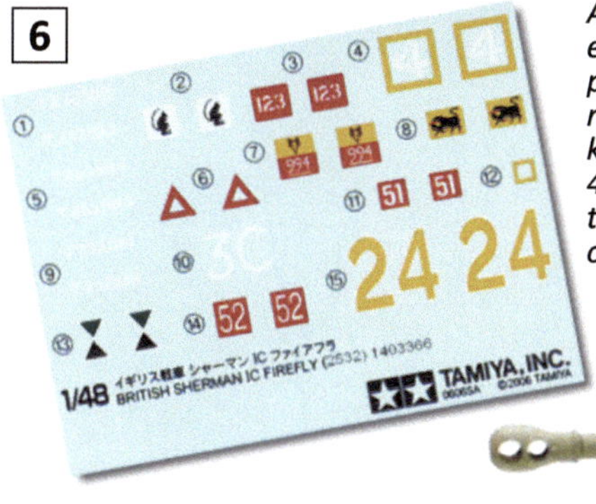

Above: 1. 1/48 scale Sherman IC Firefly. 2 and 3. 1/48 scale M4A1 and M4 kits. Both tanks were employed by the British Army with appropriate modifications. 4. 1/35 scale Firefly turret built with photo-etched and resin details from Eduard Model Accessories. 5. 1/48 scale M4 completed with metal and resin parts from Royal Model. 6. The markings sheet included with 1/48 scale Firefly IC kit. Units represented are 3/4th County of London Yeomanry, 4/7th Royal Dragoon Guards, 23rd Hussars and the East Riding Yeomanry - the latter open to question.

Above: Tamiya's limited edition VC Firefly kit, also shown at right, comes with six infantry figures. This is a re-boxing of the Tasca model first released in 2007.

TASCA/ASUKA MODEL

Rebranded as Asuka Model in 2013, this Japanese company has retained a number of the old Tasca Sherman models from its catalogue although the exceptional Sherman III kits with direct vision and cast hoods appear to have been dropped from production. In 2014 Tamiya released a re-boxed Tasca VC Firefly as a set with six infantry figures and there was some speculation at the time that they may have taken over all the Tasca moulds. However, the current Asuka catalogue shows the 1/35 scale Sherman V and the IC and VC Firefly as still available. The company's Sherman II depicts a tank with the early direct vision slots in service in North Africa but could with some modification represent a tank in use in North-west Europe. Asuka also produces a number of Sherman suspension upgrades coupled with Modelkasten flexible tracks. These models are some of the most accurate Sherman replicas available.

Above, left: Asuka's M4A1 kit. Although boxed as a US Army tank, these vehicles were employed by the British as the Sherman II and with some additions, as explained in the technical section, this would build into a suitable model. At right: The Firefly VC model built straight from the box as per the instructions using the markings provided. Below: The Sherman V kit. At right: The waterslide transfers for the Firefly IC and Firefly VC. Both are accurate for the period.

EDUARD MODEL ACCESSORIES

Founded in 1989 this Czech company produces high quality photo-etched brass detail sets and a number of scale models. Currently available are photo-etched detail sets for Tamiya's VC Firefly in 1/35 scale and IC Firefly, M4A1 and M4 in 1/48 scale. In addition there are photo-etched sets for the Dragon IC Firefly and Sherman V in 1/35 scale although the Dragon Sherman III sets have unfortunately been discontinued at this time. Eduard also offers generic brass Sherman headlight guards in 1/35 scale and sets of vinyl masks to assist with painting the wheels of Tamiya and Dragon Sherman kits in both 1/35 and 1/48 scale. The company also produces a complete kit of the M4A1 with photo-etched details and extensive marking options, although these are all for tanks of the US Army.

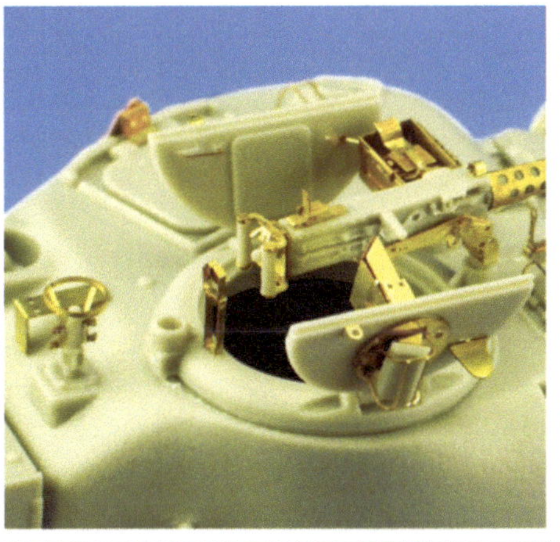

Above, left to right: Tamiya 1/48 scale Firefly VC. Dragon Models 1/35 scale Firefly VC. Tamiya 1/35 scale Firefly VC. The complicated-looking pieces of equipment fixed to the lower hull between the rear axles on the engine access door are electrically operated smoke emitters. The right-hand box is shown in the open position as it would appear after discharging its smoke candles. Below: Two views of the Dragon 1/35 scale Firefly IC built with Eduard's detail set.

Below, left to right: Dragon Models' M4A2 built with the Eduard photo-etched set. Although the detail set for the Sherman III has been discontinued, this is a viable alternative. The Tamiya 1/48 scale M4 Sherman. Dragon's 1/35 scale Firefly IC kit.

ROYAL MODELS

This Italian company has been producing high-quality accessories and aftermarket parts since the early 1990s under the guidance of its founder, Roberto Reale. The catalogue includes complete upgrade sets in 1/35 scale for the Dragon Firefly and in 1/48 scale for the Tamiya M4. There are also sets for small details such as the bogies and hatch periscopes as shown here.

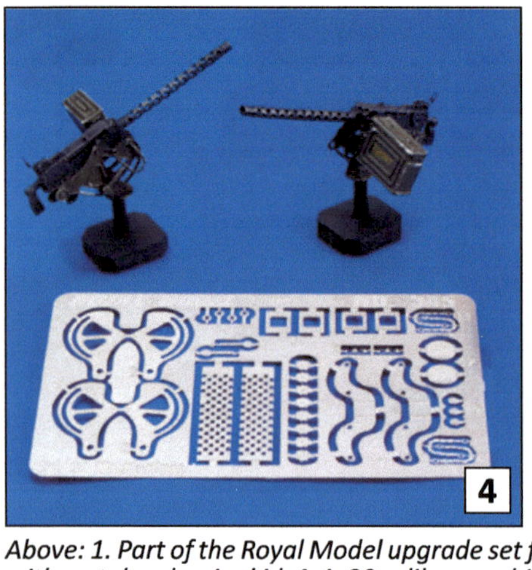

Above: 1. Part of the Royal Model upgrade set for Dragon's Firefly VC. 2. The Firefly turret armoured extension in 1/35 scale. 3. Sherman bogie with metal and resin skid. 4. A .30 calibre machine gun complete kit in 1/48 scale. 5. Part of the upgrade set for the Tamiya M4 model. 6. Detail of a built and painted 1/35 scale US M4A3 showing Royal Models .50 calibre ammunition belts.

RESICAST

Based in Belgium, Resicast produces complete kits and highly-detailed conversion sets in 1/35 scale of mostly British Army subjects. Although the company's catalogue is quite extensive, many items seem to be out of production or at least unavailable at this time.

Below: Resicast's kit for the Sherman II Duplex Drive tank. This is the so-called 'defrocked' version with the canvas screen removed. The company also offers a kit with the lowered screen in place. At right, top: A completed Sherman III model incorporating the Resicast wading stack conversion set. At right, centre: Detail of the conversion kit for the Sherman ARV Mk I.

ABER

This Polish company has been manufacturing and selling upgrade sets since 1995, working in photo-etched brass, milled aluminium and brass, stainless steel and even wood. For some time now Tamiya has included a number of Aber products with their models. Although the company's list of accessories is extensive, those items dedicated to the Sherman are quite limited. The images shown here are, from left to right, parts of the upgrade set for the Tamiya 1/48 scale M4, the highly detailed and accurate 17pdr barrel and muzzle brake in turned aluminium and brass and the brass detail set for a .50 calibre machine gun both in 1/35 scale.

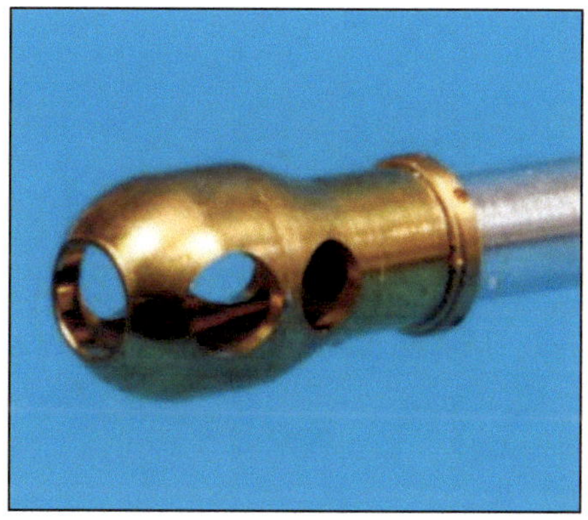

HAULER

Based in the Czech Republic, this company produces accessory sets in photo-etched brass and resin in 1/48, 1/35 and even 1/87 scale. At the time of writing the company's catalogue offered photo-etched sets for the Sherman M4, M4A1, M4A4 and a specific British set. It should be noted that most of these sets are intended to upgrade US Army and Marine Corps models of the Sherman and additional items would be required to complete British versions. Hauler also produces an accessory set for the 1/72 scale Armourfast M4 model. It appears that the 1/48 scale Duckbill track extenders shown here are no longer in production although some retailers do have stock at the time of writing.

Above, from left to right: Photo-etched end connectors fitted to T48 rubber chevron tracks. The Hauler detail set for the Tamiya M4. The photo-etched detail set for the Tamiya Firefly IC. All the items are for 1/48 scale models.

ACCURATE ARMOUR

Based in Glasgow, this company produces a line of accessory sets and complete kits with a heavy emphasis on the British and Commonwealth armies, of both the 1939-45 period and modern day. Upgrade sets are available for the Firefly and Sherman I with spoked and pressed metal wheel sets, 17pdr shells and ammunition containers. They are also a major outlet for the products from Canadian company Ultracast. Shown below are the detail set for the 1/35 scale Firefly, a Porpoise ammunition sled and a close-up of one of the wooden 17pdr ammunition crates.

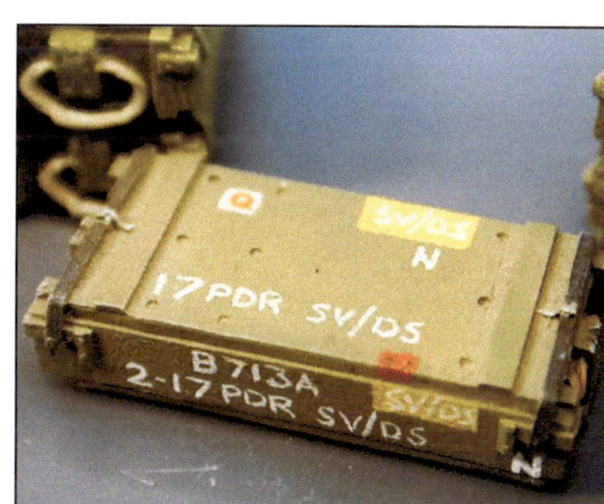

E. T. MODELS

E.T. Models, a relatively new manufacturer from China, produce upgrade sets in 1/72 and 1/35 scale in brass and resin. The detail set marketed for the Dragon IC Firefly based on the Sherman I hybrid hull shown here is the only product from the company's catalogue for a specifically British tank and contains parts made from resin, photo-etched brass and aluminium. Most of these parts could in fact be used for the Firefly IC based on the welded hull, the VC and of course the Sherman I and Sherman V. The company also offers an upgrade set for the Dragon Models US Army M4.

RB MODEL

RB Model from Poland produce a range of milled aluminium and brass gun barrels and resin accessories for 1/35 scale armour models. Shown below, from left to right, are ammunition for the Firefly's 17pdr gun in 1/48 scale, highly detailed and accurate British wireless antenna fittings in 1/35 scale and the detail set for a .50 calibre machine gun with inset, appropriate spent casings in 1/35 scale.

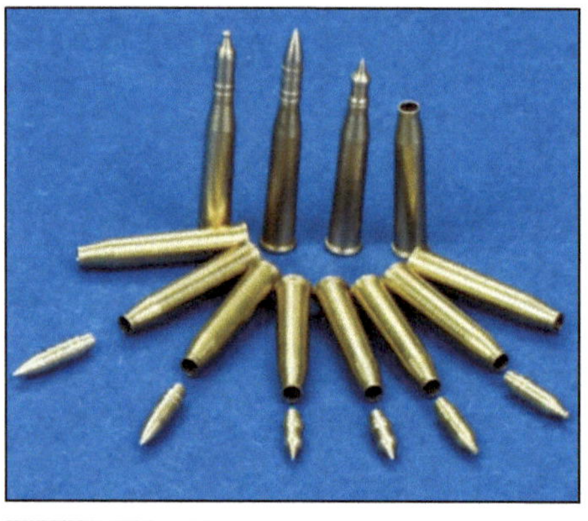

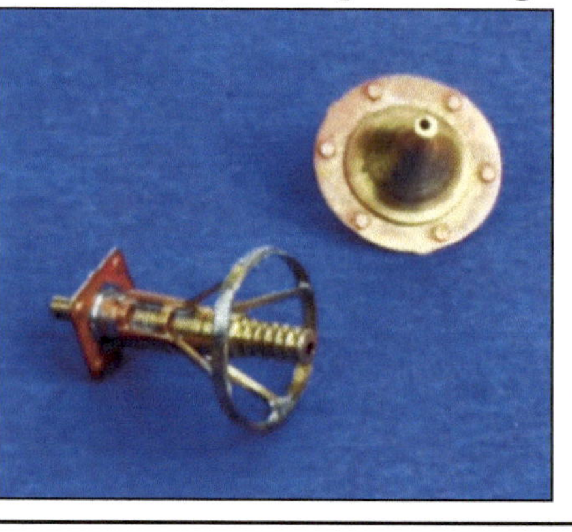

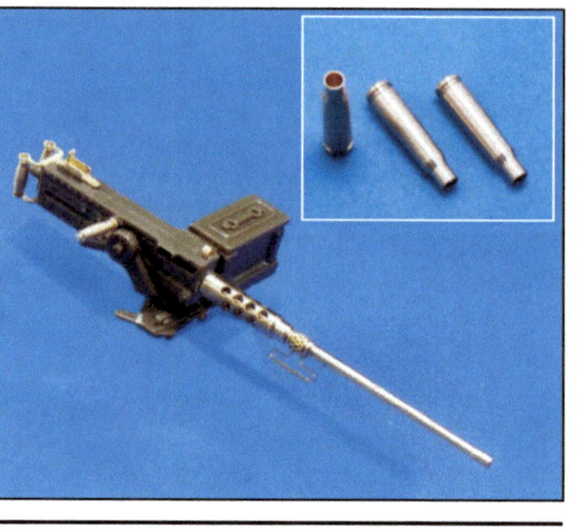

BLACK DOG

Based in the Czech Republic this company produces a large range of detailed resin accessory and upgrade sets for armoured vehicles in 1/35, 1/48 and 1/72 scale and a small number of complete kits. The items shown here are: 1. A baggage set for the 1/35 scale Firefly IC. 2. The same set with Hessian camouflage tape. 3. A more extensive camouflage in 1/48 scale. Black Dog also manufactures photo-etched brass sets in 1/35 and 1/48 scale suitable for dioramas including ferns and leaves and iron fences and railings.

VOYAGER

Voyager have been manufacturing upgrade sets for scale models since 2003 with the release of their first photo-etched brass set for 1/35 and 1/48 scale armour. The highly detailed set for the 1/35 scale Firefly includes the fittings for the so-called 'Houseboat' - a canvas cover that was intended to make the tank look like a lorry - with resin periscopes, metal towing cable and even a lucky horseshoe in brass. The detail set for the Dragon Sherman III does include items that were only seen on Shermans used in and North Africa and Italy although these could be easily replaced.

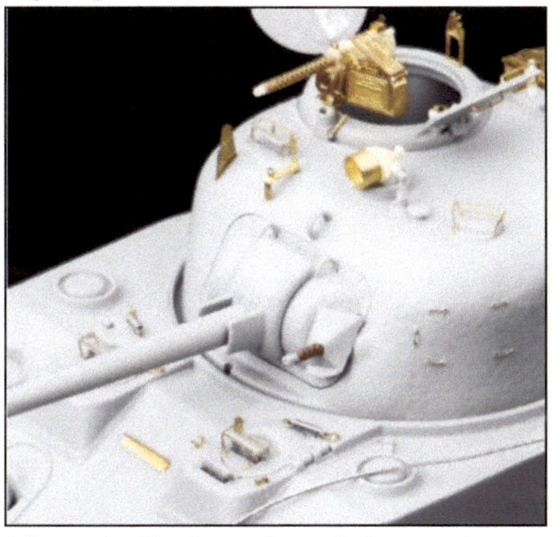

Above, left to right: Sherman Firefly detail set in 1/35 scale. The Houseboat fitting are the metal 'arms' over each front fender and the brackets on the hull side. Some of the photo-ecthed details applied to the Dragon Sherman III. Photo-etched brass details for the Tamiya 1/48 scale M4 model.

TANK WORKSHOP

This US company produces a huge range of resin upgrade parts, mostly appropriate for the 1939-45 period, with some sets for modern tanks and armoured vehicles. Their ranges of 1/35 and 1/48 scale kits include many specifically designed for British Army vehicles and an even greater number to fit US Army types. For any reader who may be interested, the business is currently being offered for sale.

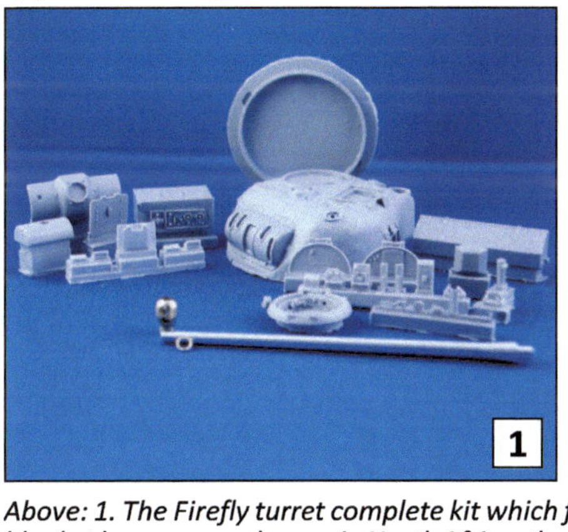

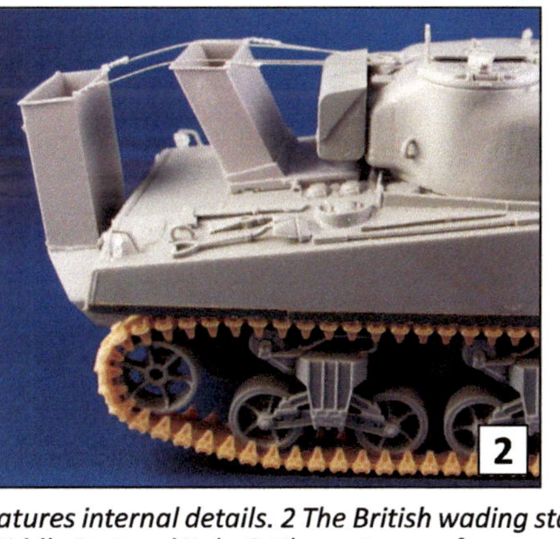

Above: 1. The Firefly turret complete kit which features internal details. 2 The British wading stacks for a Sherman III. Note that this kit has the blanket box commonly seen in North Africa, the Middle East and Italy. 3. The waterproof canvas cover for the tank's main gun.

MODELKASTEN

This Japanese company produces injection-moulded plastic track sets in 1/35 scale. For the Sherman tank Modelkasten offers sets for the T48, T49, T51, T54E1 and T62 track types. The individual links in the set for the T48 tracks are moulded with extended end connectors, commonly called duckbills. All the track types and features are covered in the technical section.

FRIULMODEL

Based in Hungary, this company produces metal track sets for the Sherman representing the T48 and T49 track types and a set marketed as 'The British Track' which is actually a T62 steel chevron track.

MARKING OPTIONS

No model is complete with out a full set of markings and, contrary to what many Axis modellers might suggest, British tanks are much more than an endless procession of Olive Drab - or perhaps more correctly Standard Camouflage Colour 15. Although most, if not all kits, come with a set of waterslide transfers, or decals to American readers, many are limited and those produced by specialist manufacturers often allow for a more unusual, even exotic, version of a particular vehicle. To give a clearer picture of the quality of the printing on some of these sheets I have shown just a portion and all contain multiple options.

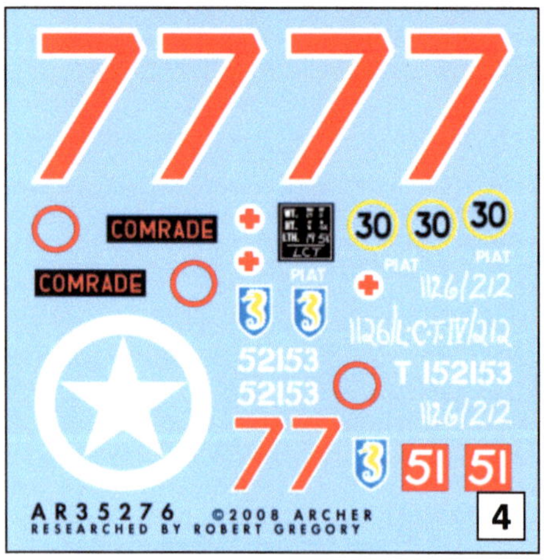

1. Archer Fine Transfers 1/35 scale waterslide transfers.
2. Star Decals (formerly Bison) 1/35 scale transfers.
3. Bison Decals 1/72 scale transfers.
4. Archer Fine Transfer 1/35 scale dry transfers.
5. Peddinghaus Decals 1/35 scale transfers.
6. Flames of War waterslide transfers for 15mm scale armour.
7. Company B markings for 1/56 scale British tanks. This is equivalent to 28mm scale.
8. Sherman III in 1/72 scale with markings from Dan Talyor Modelworks.

At left: The Italeri 1/56 scale Sherman M4 kit fitted with the metal S&S Firefly conversion set. To date, Italeri is the only major manufacturer to venture into this wargame scale.

The four independent armoured brigades were organised similarly to those attached to armoured divisions and indeed all, with the exception of 33rd Armoured Brigade, had at some time been part of larger armoured formations. They were viewed as a general reserve to be controlled at Army level and all four brigades were equipped with Sherman tanks. The number and type of tank allocated in June 1944 can see seen on page 6. Although the War Office considered that the role of the armoured brigades was not one of infantry support, this being left to the Churchill tanks of the Tank Brigades, by 1944 any doctrinal distinction between the two had disappeared and the only difference that remained was in their equipment. This was emphasised further by Montgomery and many of his commanders who were former 8th Army soldiers and considered the Sherman to be capable of both mobile and close support operations. As many of these units took part in the operations already described in the section dealing with the armoured divisions I will not repeat the tactical aspects of each here.

4th Armoured Brigade. Comprising The Royal Scots Greys (2nd Dragoons), 3rd County of London Yeomanry and 44th Royal Tank Regiment with 2nd Battalion King's Royal Rifle Corps serving as the motor battalion.

In June 1944, the regiments of 4th Armoured Brigade were equipped in the main with Sherman II tanks and Sherman VC Fireflies, each troop having one of the latter. Elements of the brigade began landing in Normandy on 7 June 1944 and were immediately sent into action to neutralise the German strongpoints around the radar station at Douvres with Centaurs of the Royal Marines and Churchill AVRE tanks of 79th Armoured Division. In late June the brigade took part in Operation Epsom and in July supported 159th Brigade and units of 15th (Scottish) Division and 53rd (Welsh) Divisions in the fighting for the Odon Bridgehead. At the end of the month, the remnants of 4th County of London Yeomanry joined the brigade forming 3rd/4th County of London Yeomanry.

In August 1944 the brigade took part in Operation Bluecoat and helped in closing the Falaise Pocket. With the bulk of the German army in Normandy trapped in the area around Falaise, 4th Armoured Brigade pushed on through Northern France into Belgium and Holland clearing German forces from the Low Countries. When the war ended 4th Armoured Brigade had made contact with the units of the Red Army advancing from the east in northern Germany.

Below: Sherman II tanks of 4th Armoured Brigade photographed in late June 1944 just prior to the commencement of Operation Epsom. Although it is not possible to identify the regiment with any certainty, the style of squadron markings and the placement of the name, Rustler, would suggest 3rd County of London Yeomanry. At far left: A Sherman II of the brigade's senior regiment, The Royal Scots Greys. Of note are the pieces of sandshield welded to the rear hull. At left: The 4th Armoured Brigade shoulder patch and the cap badge of the Greys.

8th Armoured Brigade. In June 1944 the brigade comprised 4th/7th Royal Dragoon Guards, 24th Lancers and the Nottinghamshire Yeomanry, more popularly known as the Sherwood Rangers. The brigade's motor battalion was 12th Battalion King's Royal Rifle Corps.

For the invasion of France, B and C Squadrons of the 4th/7th Dragoon Guards were both equipped with Sherman II Duplex Drive (DD) tanks landing on King sector, Gold Beach in support of 50th (Northumbrian) Division. The Sherwood Rangers' B and C Squadrons were also equipped with DD tanks based on the Sherman II, although many of these were exchanged for Sherman III tanks within days of the landing. All the Duplex Drive tanks had been delivered directly from the USA without modification. Unusually, the squadrons of 24th Lancers grouped their Fireflies together instead of following the official allocation of one tank per troop. This meant that 4th Troop of A Squadron was composed of three Fireflies as was 2nd Troop of B Squadron and 5th Troop of C Squadron. In addition each squadron headquarters was able to field one 17pdr-armed tank giving a total of twelve Fireflies for the regiment. As the reserve regiment of the brigade the 24th Lancers had no DD tanks. On D-Day, 4th/7th Royal Dragoon Guards supported the 69th Infantry Brigade, attacking towards Riviére and the Sherwood Rangers Yeomanry supported the 231st Infantry Brigade at Le Hamel. The 24th Lancers were held in reserve to be landed later in the afternoon but due to the deteriorating weather and the congestion on the beaches they did not land until the following day. The brigade was involved in the fighting for Putot-en-Bessin and in the area of Villers-Bocage. and in the fierce battles near Rauray at the end of July, where the 24th Lancers were so badly battered that the regiment was disbanded and replaced by the 13th/18th Hussars. During the first two weeks of August 4th/7th Royal Dragoon Guards and the Sherwood Rangers supported 43rd (Wessex) Division and took part in the capture of Jurques, south-east of Villers-Bocage and the fighting for Le Plessis Grimault further to the south-west where the brigade was able to claim the capture of a Tiger II. During this time the Hussars were attached to 50th (Northumbrian) Division for the assault on Amaye-sur-Suelles, between Caumont-l'Évente and Villers-Bocage. By the end of the month, with the German units in Normandy trapped at Falaise, the brigade had reached the Seine at Vernon and was ordered to strike west and open a route to the Somme for the Guards Armoured Division.

After the Normandy campaign the brigade fought in Belgium, Holland and northern Germany.

Sherman III tanks of 4th/7th Royal Dragoon Guards, the senior regiment of 8th Armoured Brigade, photographed near Raura on 28 June 1944. Photographic evidence would suggest that the large turret numbers seen here were not used by all the tanks of this regiment and the significance of the system is not known at this time. These large red numbers, outlined in white have in fact have caused some vehicles to be incorrectly described as belonging to 13th/18th Hussars. The composite 8th Armoured Brigade formation badge and AoS sign is clearly visible on the right side of the rear hull. The white bar used to indicate Army troops has been rendered as a thin white line under the unit serial number 994 and this was common throughout the brigade.

A Sherman II Duplex Drive (DD) tank passing through Douet, near Bayeux, on 25 June 1944. The formation badge of 8th Armoured Brigade is just visible at the centre of the hull glacis directly between the driver and lap gunner's positions. Although the AoS number is not clear enough to identify the regiment, the cap badges of 4th/7th Royal Dragoon Guards are visible in the original print. Many DD crews removed the floatation screen soon after the landings as it could be set alight by the fire from the hull machine gun.

A Sherman VC Firefly of 24th Lancers, the second senior regiment of 8th Armoured Brigade, photographed near St. Leger on 11 June 1944. This tank is also shown in the illustration section on page 22.

Lance Corporal James and Sergeant Coe of C Squadron, 144th RAC, proudly display a German flag captured during the attack on Caen on 10 July 1944. The large call sign numbers were indicative of the tanks of 27th Armoured Brigade and may have been rendered in the colours denoting regimental seniority. The curve of the hull front of this Sherman I Hybrid and the larger lap gunner's hatch, set at an angle, can be seen here.

27th Armoured Brigade. The brigade's senior regiment, 13th/18th Royal Hussars, landed on Sword Beach on the morning of 6 June 1944 with the DD tanks of A and B Squadron supporting 1st Battalion Suffolk Regiment and No 4 Commando. The regiment's C Squadron landed last with the brigade's ammunition reserve carried on waterproof sledges.

The Staffordshire Yeomanry came ashore with the regiments of 185th Infantry Brigade and moved inland with the infantry riding on their tanks. The brigade's junior regiment, East Riding Yeomanry, landed later in the day with the 9th Brigade of 3rd Infantry Division. One troop of 13th/18th Hussars were assigned to protect 21st Army Group headquarters and it seems that their tanks, or at least the Fireflies, were never returned to the regiment. Throughout the month of June the brigade took part in the fighting along the Orne River and the attempts to capture Caen.

As part of Operation Goodwood, the brigade supported 3rd Infantry Division in its attacks on the German defences around Troarn, east of Caen on the main road to Rouen.

On 30 July 1944 the brigade was disbanded with 13th/18th Hussars taking over the vehicles of the Staffordshire Yeomanry and replacing 24th Lancers in 8th Armoured Brigade and the East Riding Yeomanry going to 33rd Armoured Brigade.

A Sherman VC Firefly of A Squadron, 1st East Riding Yeomanry, the junior regiment of 27th Armoured Brigade, photographed on 1 June 1944 when it was loaded onto its LST for the trip to Normandy. This tank is depicted in the illustration section on page 23

Also shown on page 3, on board a landing ship heading towards Normandy, Balaclava, *a Sherman III of regimental headquarters, 13th/18th Royal Hussars, fires on German troops using the Horsa gliders in the background as cover near Ranville on 10 June 1944. This vehicle is also shown and discussed in the colour section on page 23.*

33rd Armoured Brigade. In June 1944 the brigade contained 1st Northamptonshire Yeomanry, 144th Regiment Royal Armoured Corps and 148th Regiment Royal Armoured Corps. These last two regiments had been raised from battalions of the East Lancashire Regiment and the Loyal Regiment (North Lancashire) respectively, both of which were infantry formations.

When the brigade first landed in Normandy its regiments were equipped with Sherman I tanks and Sherman VC Fireflies, the latter allocated one per troop. The brigade took part in the fighting around Caen and Operation Charnwood. On 16 July, together with Churchill Crocodile flamethrowing tanks from 79th Armoured Division, the brigade supported units of 59th (Staffordshire) Infantry Division as part of Operation Pomegranate, in an assault launched to divert German attention away from the upcoming Operation Goodwood. Following the capture of Caen the brigade was attached to Canadian II Corps for Operation Totalise, the attack towards the town of Falaise and, in early August, the attempt to close the resulting pocket.

During this time the tanks of the Northamptonshire Yeomanry were involved in an action which has since become one of the most well known, and controversial, engagements of the campaign. On the morning of 8 August the regiment had reached the village of Saint-Aignan-de-Cramesnil, south of Caen, and while B Squadron remained in the village the other two squadrons moved further south into the cover of a wooded area overlooking the Caen-Falaise road. Very soon German tanks could be seen advancing along the road from the direction of the town of Cintheaux. The British tankers were ordered to hold their fire until the Germans were well within range. The German force was commanded by SS-Hauptsturmführer Michael Wittmann who had become something of a celebrity in Germany. As as the German tanks approached Gaumesnil, moving through the open country on either side of the road they were completely unaware of the British Sherman tanks which now opened a devastating fire. Positioned at the rear of the German formation, Wittmann's command tank was hit by two rounds that slammed into the side of his Tiger near the fuel tank, causing an explosion of such force that the turret was lifted from the hull. Within seconds the tank's ammunition exploded blowing the turret completely clear of the vehicle and ripping off both tracks. Of the other six tanks, five were knocked out and the last abandoned. The German press claimed that Wittman's tank had been knocked out by Allied fighter-bombers and for years this version was accepted. However in recent times it has been claimed that the Tiger was knocked by either a Firefly of A Squadron's 3 Troop although there is some evidence that a tank of 27th Canadian Armoured Regiment, which was positioned to the east of the road, may have been responsible (1).

On 16 August 148th Regiment Royal Armoured Corps, which had been badly depleted by the battles of July, was disbanded and replaced by the East Riding Yeomanry. By the end of 1944 the brigade had given up its Shermans and been re-equipped with Buffalo amphibious tractors and Kangaroo personnel carriers and to 79th Armoured Division.

An M3 Honey command tank and Sherman I of 144th RAC, 33rd Armoured Brigade photographed on 8 July 1944 during Operation Charnwood. The Sherman is shown and discussed in the illustration section on page 25. Note that the M3 still has the wading stack fixed to the rear hull.

1. The Northamptonshire Yeomanry Firefly was commanded by Sergeant Douglas Gordon, who was wounded in the exchange of fire. The tank's gunner, Trooper Joe Ekins, claimed that he had hit three of the Tigers although he had no idea at the time who Wittman was. The story first surfaced in 1985 in a magazine article written by Les Taylor, who had served in the regiment and was supported by the historian Ken Tout, also a former Yeoman. That Wittman was killed in this action is beyond doubt and although we may never know who was responsible, much of the criticism of Taylor's claim rests heavily on the way the story was subsequently reported in the British Press where the original article was padded out with numerous fantasies, none of which emanated from either Taylor, Tout or Ekins.

While most regiments of the Royal Artillery used vehicles that could fairly be described as armoured, this list is restricted to those units known to have been equipped with Sherman Artillery Observation Post (AOP) tanks. These were Sherman gun tanks were the main armament had been replaced by a wooden, dummy gun allowing extra radio equipment to be installed in the turret (1). Field regiments with self-propelled guns, either the Priest or Sexton, were allocated a total of thirteen AOP tanks, although this number does not tally with the official organisation which calls for one tank for the regiment's headquarters, one for each battery commander and two tanks for each troop. I suspect that in practice the regimental command had two tanks with one tank for each battery headquarters and two tanks for the troops of just two batteries. As far as possible I have endeavoured to use the correct and full title of each regiment although at times these are somewhat cumbersome. The abbreviation TA at the end of a regiment's name indicates that the unit raised from the Territorial Army and the letters RA of course stand for Royal Artillery. This list is far from definitive as detailed records are not available as they are for the Royal armoured Corps and some entries are admittedly based on photographic evidence only.

3rd Regiment Royal Horse Artillery.
This regiment originally consisted of two Batteries, D/J and M/P, later reformed as D, J and M, all batteries of the RHA being referred to by letters. During the Normandy battles, 3rd Royal Horse Artillery was the senior field regiment of 7th Armoured Division. The regiment operated Sexton 25pdr self-propelled guns and Sherman AOP tanks.

5th Regiment Royal Horse Artillery.
Made up of Batteries G and K, this regiment was attached to 7th Armoured Division. Although officially equipped with Cromwell AOP tanks, there is photographic evidence that at least one Sherman V was on hand with the regimental headquarters

13th Regiment Royal Horse Artillery (Honourable Artillery Company) (TA).
Although this unit is mentioned in this book as being equipped with Sherman AOP tanks, they were not received until late 1944.

33rd Field Regiment, RA.
Attached to the 3rd Infantry Division and containing Batteries 101, 109 and 113/114, this regiment was re-equipped with 105mm Priest self-propelled guns and Sherman AOP tanks in May 1944 in preparation for the Normandy landings. A tank of this regiment is shown in the illustration section on page 28.

76th (Highland) Field Regiment, RA (TA).
Attached to the 3rd Infantry Division and comprising Batteries 302, 303 and 454 - with 304 (City of Dundee) Battery joining the regiment just prior to D-Day. Sources differ as to when this regiment was converted to the self-propelled role, but there is solid photographic evidence that the regiment had at least some 105mm Priest self-propelled guns and Sherman V AOP tanks on hand prior to the first landings in Normandy.

86th (East Anglian, Hertfordshire Yeomanry) Field Regiment, RA (TA).
Formed from the Hertfordshire Yeomanry and made up of Batteries 341 (St Albans), 342 (Hertford) and 462. Prior to D-Day the regiment was re-equipped as a self-propelled unit operating both 105mm Priests and 25pdr Sextons supported by Sherman V AOP tanks and special tactics were developed including firing from landing craft at sea. In June 1944, as 2nd Army troops, the regiment was attached to 8th Armoured Brigade. The markings of this regiment are shown in the illustration section on page 28.

90th (City of London) Field Regiment, RA (TA).
Made up of Batteries 357 (1st City of London), 358 (2nd City of London) and 465 this regiment was attached to 50th Infantry Division until November 1944. Prior to the invasion the regiment was equipped with 25pdr Sexton self-propelled guns and Sherman V AOP tanks.

147th (Essex Yeomanry) Field Regiment, RA (TA).
Formed from 413 Battery, 104th (Essex Yeomanry) Regiment, RHA. This regiment was equipped as a self-propelled unit by May 1944 coming under the command of 2nd Army. In June 1944 the regiment was supporting 8th Armoured Brigade during which time it used the Brigade's formation badge - returning to 2nd Army control in late 1944. There is some evidence that the regiment operated a number of Sherman AOP tanks.

153rd (Leicestershire Yeomanry) Field Regiment, RA (TA).
Formed from 129, 130 and 131 Batteries the regiment was equipped with 25pdr Sextons and Sherman V AOP tanks by May 1944 This regiment served as the junior field artillery regiment of Guards Armoured Division until the war's end. A tank of this regiment is shown and discussed further on page 17 of the illustration section.

Following page, at top: Carriers and a Sherman AOP tank waiting to cross the Orne river during Operation Goodwood on 18 July 1944. The AoS sign of the number 77 on a red over blue square denotes an anti-tank regiment attached to an armoured division while the small Royal Artillery tactical sign above that identifies the commander of the 3rd Battery's G Troop. The markings on the Sherman indicate that this tank is operated by the senior Field Artillery Regiment of an Armoured Division and has been allocated to the commander of E troop of the regiment's 3rd Battery. These markings are explained further in the appendices at the end of this book. Inset: A Sherman V AOP of 5th Royal Horse Artillery attached to 7th Armoured Division. The Royal Artillery tactical sign in front of the driver's position is unusual and possibly identifies the regiment's second in command although there was no official authorisation for an AOP for that officer. At bottom: A Sherman V AOP from 33rd Field Regiment of 3rd Infantry Division photographed on 6 June 1944. This tank and its markings are discussed on page 28 of the illustration section.

1. As with most aspects of the British Army there were exceptions to this rule and an example of an AOP with a functioning gun can see seen on page 5. The author and historian Patrick Delaforce, who served with 13th Regiment Royal Horse Artillery of 11th Armoured Division, is adamant that the AOP tanks of his regiment all had functioning guns.

RG
77

Very few photographs of the Royal Marine's Sherman V tanks are known to have survived and to my knowledge all but one are reproduced in this book, with the exception of the film that was used to create the illustration on page 27. The tanks seen here were photographed near Tilly-sur-Seulles on 13 June 1944.

Formed in early 1943 in anticipation of the landings in France, this formation consisted of 1st Royal Marine Armoured Support Regiment, 2nd Royal Marine Armoured Support Regiment and 5th Royal Marine (Independent) Armoured Support Battery.

The two regiments were each made up of two batteries, numbered from 1 to 4. Each battery contained four troops which were referred to as A, B, C and D for 1st Battery, E, F, G and H for 2nd Battery, P, Q, S and T for 3rd battery and W, X, Y and Z for 4th Battery. The troops of the independent 5th Battery were designated R, S, T and V. From the available photographs it appears that each tank was named to correspond with the troop letter. Each troop contained two Centaurs and a Sherman OP tank giving a total of twenty Sherman and eighty Centaur tanks for the entire group. Although, as we shall see, the batteries did not field all their allotted tanks on D-Day. The group, regiment and battery headquarters had no tanks, their purpose being to command and ensure an adequate supply of ammunition. Each troop was divided into a Left Section and a Right Section, each of two Centaurs and both sections were controlled by the troop commander from a Sherman tank. Each section landed in a LCT(A) with the Shermans landing with the Left Section (1). Personnel included officers and gunner-drivers seconded from the Royal Artillery and maintenance and repairs were carried out by fitters and mechanics from the Royal Armoured Corps. The majority of the crews were, however, Royal Marine gunners some of who had been trained to operate the guns of the Royal Navy's ships.

This group was originally intended as a purely assault formation and was expected to be withdrawn from the invasion area within 24 hours of the first landings. Consequently it was decided that the Centaurs' engines would be removed to allow space for extra ammunition. However, on an inspection tour in February 1944 King George VI, accompanied by General Montgomery, asked when the tanks would land and was informed that they would not, as they had no means of moving. Concerned that these engine-less tanks might block the invasion beaches in the first, vital hours, Montgomery ordered that the engines be replaced. On 6 June, 5th Battery supported the units assaulting Sword Beach with sixteen Centaur and four Sherman OP tanks. All the tanks were ashore by the early hours of the following morning with the exception of two Centaurs and a single Sherman whose landing craft returned to England with the tanks on board. The 2nd Support Regiment with twenty-six Centaurs and seven Sherman tanks landed at least one troop on Juno Beach by the evening of the first day. One LCT(A) was lost with all its vehicles. The tanks of the 1st Regiment supported the units landing on Gold Beach, losing a Sherman OP tank to enemy fire as it left its landing craft.

As mentioned above, this formation was solely intended to provide fire support on the invasion beaches but these tanks soldiered on for almost three weeks after the landings, the group's maintenance personnel performing near-miracles to keep them running. The surviving Centaurs were finally passed to 1st Canadian Centaur Battery, 53rd Light Artillery Regiment's X (Armoured) Battery and 27th Light Anti-Aircraft Regiment's 6th Battery. A number were also handed over to the French 13.Regiment de Dragons. What became of the Sherman OP tanks is unknown.

The markings used by the Royal Marines are described and shown in the illustration section on pages 27 and 28.

1. LCT(A) - Landing Craft, Tank (Assault).

ROYAL MARINE ARMOURED SUPPORT GROUP, 6 JUNE 1944

RMASG GROUP HEADQUARTERS
Group commander, Brigadier D.C.W. Sanders, Royal Artillery
Group deputy commander, Colonlel A.J. Harvey, Royal Marines

The HQ staff contained one artillery officer and six officers of the Royal Marines. The medical officer and chaplain were both supplied by the Royal Navy.

HEADQUARTERS WING AND HOLDING BATTERY

Commanded by a major and ten officers of the Royal Marines. The five officers in charge of maintenance were all seconded from the Royal Armoured Corps, as were the sixty-five mechanics. The battery contained thirty RM gunners and five RA drivers as reserves. A further sixteen Marines provided general assistance to the officers.

1st ROYAL MARINE ARMOURED SUPPORT REGIMENT

Commander, lieutenant colonel, RM
Adjutant, captain, RM
Signals NCO

- **1st BATTERY**: A Troop, B Troop, C Troop, D Troop
- **2nd BATTERY**: E Troop, F Troop, G Troop, H Troop

Troop HQ: OP
1st Section: Centaur 1, Centaur 2
2nd Section: Centaur 3, Centaur 4

2nd ROYAL MARINE ARMOURED SUPPORT REGIMENT

- **3rd BATTERY**: J Troop, K Troop, L Troop, M Troop
- **4th BATTERY**: N Troop, O Troop, P Troop, Q Troop

5th (Independent) BATTERY: R Troop, S Troop, T Troop, V Troop

The troop commander controlled the troop from the Sherman OP while the troop second-in-command was with Centaur 3. A sergeant major commanded Centaur 1 and the other tanks were commanded by sergeants, although in practice the position was often filled by a corporal. Each section was transported on an LCT (A) with two Centaurs positioned side by side at the front and the Sherman OP of the troop commander accompanied the 1st Section. An ammunition team of one NCO and four ammunition handlers was included in each ship and some of these teams remained with the tanks after 6 June, although most returned to England.

Another photograph of the 2nd Battery tank shown on the previous page. The RAC red-white-red flash on the hull side is clearly visible in this image. This vehicle is also shown and discussed in the illustration section on page 26.

Before they were issued to combat or training units each tank underwent modifications seen as necessary for the efficiency and comfort of British tank crews. These included a stowage bin or blanket box fitted to the turret rear, brackets to hold spare track links, fire extinguishers which were clamped on either side of the hull towards the rear and additional towing lugs used to secure the deep wading gear. Some, but not all, tanks had a smoke emitter fitted to the engine access doors. Other modifications are shown in the accompanying photographs. Listed here are the major models and variants of the Sherman employed by the British Army in North-west Europe and the Normandy Campaign.

Sherman I (M4) and Sherman I Hybrid (M4 Composite). Produced from July 1942 until January 1944, Britain received a total of 2,096 Sherman I models, including the composite hull versions. The initial welded hull was designed with the front glacis plate inclined at an angle of 57 degrees and featured two box-like extensions, referred to as hoods, which incorporated hatches for the driver and assistant driver. In the British Army the assistant driver was known as the lap gunner. During production the direct vision slots (1) in front of the two hull positions were at first welded shut and then removed from production and replaced with fixed periscopes (2). An antenna bracket was welded onto the right hand side of the glacis (3) and the shape and construction of these varied between manufacturers. On early models the final drives and differential were protected by a three piece armoured cover (4) that was bolted together. This was later replaced by a cast, single piece version (5). The rear hull plate (6) was distinguished by an inverted u-shaped cut out and this partially covered the air filtering system (7). Two hinged doors at the rear of the hull gave access to the engine (8). The composite hull, with its cast front (9), was seen as a solution to production delays and the high costs experienced with the all-welded process. As the welding of the hull front accounted for most of the production time, the firm of Chrysler suggested that a cast front be fitted to the M4 hull and in August 1943 full-scale production began. Many, if not all, these tanks featured improvements which were being incorporated into production including appliqué armour (10) on the hull sides, a gun travel lock on the glacis and the cast differential housing. A number would have been fitted with the turret with the pistol port. The first fifty production vehicles were built with the small hatches of the M4.

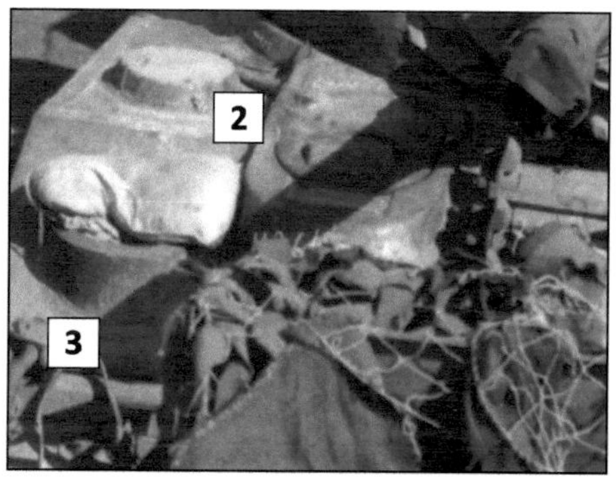

The cast turret was armed with a 75mm M3 main gun and .30 calibre machine gun. The turret had a cupola for the commander and a pistol port on the left hand side (11). In April 1943 it was decide to delete the pistol port from production but this was so unpopular with the troops in the field that it was reinstated in July. A number of pistol ports were welded closed before the new order was issued. As with all models of the Sherman tank, early production vehicles were fitted with the M34 gun mantlet (12) until its replacement with the M34A1 version (13) in March 1943. All vehicles were powered by a Wright 9-cylinder gasoline engine. Following British advice, gained through combat experience, the radio was installed in the turret and not in the hull as had been the initial American practice.

Sherman II (M4A1). This version was the first model of the Sherman to enter British service and is easily distinguished by its one-piece, cast hull (1). Although the hoods for the driver and lap gunner are contoured into the hull (2), the outward opening hatches were identical to those of the welded-hull Sherman I. The engine access doors and air filters were also the same and the rear hull plate featured a very shallow cut out. From January 1944 a small number were built with the so-called large hatch and some of these were delivered to Britain as Duplex Drive conversions (3), operating with 8th Armoured Brigade in Normandy. All were equipped with a Continental R-975 air-cooled radial engine.

Sherman III (M4A2). The welded hull of this model was similar in appearance to the early Sherman I with the most obvious differences being the engine access doors on the rear deck behind the turret, the exhaust systems for the diesel engine and the rear hull plate which was much larger, without any cut out and was sloped towards the rear (4). When the direct vision blocks were dropped from production, tanks were manufactured with angular, welded driver's and lap gunner's hoods (5) and also cast hoods that were angled at the side (6). Both were identifying features of this model. The example shown here also has the distinctive D-shaped, welded antenna bracket (7). All Sherman III tanks were fitted with twin General Motors diesel engines and indeed were often referred to in early British reports as simply *'Sherman, diesel'*. In numbers received they were second only to the Sherman V with a total of 5,033 being delivered.

Sherman V (M4A4). Although outwardly similar to the Sherman I, the M4A4 hull was built some 6 inches longer to accommodate the massive Chrysler 5-line engine. A slightly modified suspension was also required and the number of track shoes was increased from seventy-nine to eighty-three. As with the other models, this tank featured the early M34 gun mount until it was replaced in March 1943 by the M34A1, the version which is most often seen in photographs of the Sherman V. The early type, three-piece differential cover was retained on all vehicles. Identifying features were the protruding hoods (8) and cast antenna bracket (9), the radiator filler on the rear deck (10) below the turret overhang and the sloped rear plate shown here (11) with the distinctive rear hull stowage box (12). This model was by far the most numerous Sherman type in service with the British Army with 7,155 vehicles being supplied by the war's end.

17pdr anti-tank gun conversions. Initially rejected as impractical and only grudgingly put into production as a stop-gap measure, the Sherman tanks fitted with the British 17pdr gun were among the most successful Allied armoured vehicles produced during the war. In order to mount the gun in the Sherman turret it was turned on its side and adapted for left hand loading. As the breech of the main gun now filled much of the turret, and allowance had to be made for the gun's recoil, an armoured extension had to be fixed to the turret rear to hold the wireless that was normally positioned behind the commander and loader (1). This armoured box, which also acted as a counterweight, is a distinguishing feature of these vehicles when viewed from the rear. As the loader's access to the turret hatch was now obstructed by the gun breech it was necessary to cut a second hatch in the turret roof (2). To increase the amount of ammunition carried, both the lap position and machine gun were removed and the aperture covered with a thick metal plate. The gun mantlet was completely redesigned (3). Conversions to mount the larger gun in place of the 75mm were carried out on using the Sherman V, Sherman I and Sherman I Hybrid models and any suggestion that 17pdr guns were fitted to other versions is incorrect. In the days prior to the invasion an attempt was made to allocate at least one 17pdr tank per troop to the armoured regiments, including the Cromwell equipped 22nd Armoured Brigade. The abbreviation *'pdr'* as applied to British and Commonwealth guns refers to the weight, in pounds, of the projectile. It should be noted that these tanks were referred to officially as either Sherman 17pdr or Sherman VC or IC, the letter C being the designation for the 17pdr armament, and although it is unlikely that the name Firefly was ever used during the war I have employed the term here and throughout this book as it will be familiar to most readers.

Duplex Drive (DD) Sherman. These tanks were enclosed in a large waterproof screen (4) made of rubberised canvas which could be raised to allow the tank to 'swim' and then lowered once ashore. To hold the screen, a mild steel platform was welded to the hull and the screen was lowered and raised by means of compressed air pumped into thirty-six large rubber tubes positioned around the hull. Once ashore many crews removed the canvas screen (5). A standard drive sprocket replaced the rear idler and this drove the two propellers which were fitted to the rear hull. A speed of 4 knots was attainable, although this was in calm water and many tanks were swamped while trying to reach the invasion beaches. The DD tanks employed in Normandy were all delivered directly from the United States and were based on the Sherman V (6) and Sherman II, an unknown number of the latter being built using the large hatch version.

Other specialist vehicles included the Sherman Crab, a mine-clearing tank operated in Normandy by the regiments of 30th Armoured Brigade. These tanks were produced in two versions and referred to as the Crab I and Crab II, the latter being a refinement of the earlier vehicle, equipped with a contouring device to better negotiate irregularities in the ground. All conversions were based on the Sherman V. An example can be seen on page 16. The Armoured Recovery Vehicles (ARV) as the name suggests were employed to recover battle-damaged or broken-down vehicles during combat. They were operated by units of the Royal Electrical and Mechanical Engineers (REME) attached to armoured and infantry formations. Produced in two versions, the Mk I and MK II, only the former served with Sherman units in North-west Europe. The majority of Sherman ARV allocated to armoured units fighting in Normandy in June 1944 were based on the Sherman V M4A4 with just twenty-seven based on Sherman III chassis. Beach Armoured Recovery Vehicles (BARV) were based on the Sherman III and were used to keep the invasion beaches clear. Operated by REME crews, these tanks could function in up to 9 foot depths and were also capable of refloating small landing craft. An example can be seen on page 37.

1. The Royal Armoured Corps. In 1939 the British Army was made up of a regular force of both full-time soldiers and reservists and the part-time volunteers of the Territorial Army. The regular Army was able to field 30 cavalry regiments and 140 infantry battalions although many reservists had been in civilian life for some years. The Territorial Army was made up of over 200 infantry and tank battalions with the mounted regiments of the Yeomanry, some of which had been mechanised. In April 1939 the regular cavalry units that had been converted to armoured regiments and the Royal Tank Corps were amalgamated to become the Royal Armoured Corps (1). By the beginning of 1944 the Royal Armoured Corps (RAC) contained the former regular cavalry regiments, including the Household Cavalry, the Regiments of Horse and the cavalry of the line, the battalions of the Royal Tank Regiment, most of the Yeomanry regiments, and a number of converted infantry battalions (2). Later that year the Royal Armoured Corps absorbed the Reconnaissance Corps.

2. The Regiment. Some explanation of the notion of a regiment may be helpful as the term, as used within the British Army, is somewhat flexible. Infantry regiments existed as administrative and training establishments, raising battalions which were then sent on active service. The battalions were numbered sequentially and also retained the name of the regiment, for example 4th Battalion The Dorsetshire Regiment. They were often named for the region or town where they were based and all were proud of their traditions. During the war a number of regular infantry battalions were converted to armoured units and came under the control of the Royal Armoured Corps. Their titles incorporated the RAC number and their original name, for example 107th RAC 5th King's Own Royal Regiment. The cavalry and Yeomanry were formed into regiments, which were similar in size to infantry battalions, and retained their individual identity and original title, for example 5th Royal Inniskilling Dragoon Guards or the Staffordshire Yeomanry, throughout their service. In a manner similar to the regiments of infantry, the Royal Tank Regiment (RTR) was made up of eight regular battalions when the war commenced, numbered from 1 to 8. A further four regular battalions were raised for the duration of the war, numbered 9 to 12, and an additional twelve battalions were formed from units of the Territorial Army and these were numbered from 40 to 51. Thus the title, 1st RTR refers to the 1st Battalion of the Royal Tank Regiment, and so on. The Royal Armoured Corps controlled the training and support establishments although as the war progressed, as mentioned above, a number of infantry formations were converted to armoured units and came under its control (3).

3. Seniority. One of the most important aspects of the British Army is the principle of seniority, or more correctly precedence. The concept dates back to the time when the entire army would parade before the monarch with the most senior unit taking the place of honour on the right flank. This is a complex subject and for our purposes I will restrict the narrative to the units of the RAC. Regiments and battalions were combined into brigades which were purely temporary formations. In general terms, seniority within the brigade was largely dependent upon when a regiment or battalion was raised, with regular army regiments and battalions taking precedence over Yeomanry and Territorial units. For example, the regular battalions of the Royal Tank Regiment, which was formed in 1916, would take precedence over a regiment of the Yeomanry but would be considered junior to the 8th King's Royal Irish Hussars, a regular cavalry regiment which traced its lineage back to 1693. This system can be the cause of some confusion to the researcher or general reader when regiments or battalions were transferred between brigades, as they often were, requiring a reorganisation of the brigade's order of battle with the requisite changes in markings, no mean feat under battle conditions. However, the notion of seniority was, and remains, one of the pillars on which the British Army is built and these impositions would have been regarded as minor, if indeed they were so regarded at all. The regiments and brigades described in the main text are all given in order of precedence.

Photographed on 11 June 1944 near St Léger, the combined AoS sign and Formation Badge identifying 24th Lancers of 8th Armoured Brigade can be seen on the hull rear plate of this Sherman VC Firefly. Note the route markers further along the road in the shape of the brigade's Fox Face insignia.

1. In case the reader should think the process went smoothly, it should be remembered that it was 1942 before the last cavalry unit, the Queens Own Yorkshire Dragoons serving in the Middle East, gave up its horses. When the reorganisation took place the Tank Corps was renamed as the Royal Tank Regiment.

2. A number of Yeomanry regiments served with the artillery.

3. The infantry battalions converted to Regiments RAC were given the choice of retaining their regimental distinctions, such as cap badges, or wearing those of the Royal Armoured Corps.

Above: Examples of various common markings. A. Bridge Classification, giving the vehicle's weight in tons. B. Formation Badge, in this case 11th Armoured Division. C. Unit Serial Number on an Arm of Service square, this example identifying the headquarters of an armoured brigade. D. Squadron Tactical Sign for B Squadron with the troop number at the centre. E. Tank's name. F. Just visible here is a patch of poison gas detection paint.

4. Markings

War Department (WD) numbers. These numbers were an individual identifier issued for all vehicles, including trailers, by the War Office. Each number was prefixed by a letter describing the type of vehicle, T in the case of a tank, and painted onto a suitable surface. The vehicle retained its WD number for the duration of its service life.

Bridge Classification Numbers. All British Army vehicles carried a sign indicating their weight class which not only determined what vehicles could use which bridge, but was also an essential aid in the recovery of damaged vehicles. The most common form this took was of a yellow circle with a black number indicating the vehicle's weight in tons.

Recognition Markings. The red/white/red RAC flash introduced in early 1942 was less commonly encountered by June 1944 and examples can be seen in the illustrations on pages 26 and 28. From July 1943 a large white star enclosed by a ring was introduced as an aerial recognition sign to replace the RAF roundel then in use. Examples applied to the rear deck and turret roof of Sherman tanks could still be seen in 1945.

Formation Badges. Officially all vehicles carried the badge of the higher formation to which they belonged, which was usually a division or an independent brigade. Often incorporating intricate and colourful features, sizes, colours and designs varied widely between formations and examples are shown in the illustration section.

Divisional Unit Serial Numbers. Often referred to today as Arm of Service signs or squares, the variations and evolution of these markings, carried on British military vehicles throughout the war, is far beyond the scope of this book. Originally conceived as a means of identification that would prove indecipherable to the enemy, these signs were made up of a divisional unit serial number painted onto a rectangle of the appropriate Arm of Service colour or colours. Officially the rectangle was to be 8 ½ inches (215mm) wide and 9 ½ inches (241mm) high, with the number being 6 inches (152mm) high. However in practice the shape could vary from the approved size to a square of between 10 and 12 inches. The divisional unit serial numbers and arm of service squares in use by armoured units during the Normandy campaign are shown and discussed in the colour illustrations.

Armoured Vehicle Tactical signs. Each squadron within the regiment was represented by a Tactical Sign. These took the form of a geometric shape painted onto the tank. Regimental HQ and the headquarters squadron was identified by a diamond, A Squadron by a triangle, B Squadron a square and C Squadron by a circle. The sequence of colours was usually red, yellow and blue indicating senior, second senior and junior regiments respectively. White was used in the case of an unbrigaded regiment. The style, size and application of these markings varied considerably and examples can be seen in the photographs and in illustration section.

Camouflage colours. All colours for use with vehicle camouflage and their application were stipulated in British Standard (BS) 381C of 1930 and BS 987C of 1942. The colours in use at the time of the Normandy Campaign and that need to concern us are :

Standard Camouflage Colour (SCC 2). Sometimes referred to as brown, khaki brown or service drab and described as a rich, dark brown tending towards khaki. Although replaced in April 1944 by SCC 15 it could be seen for some time after that as paints were customarily used until stocks were exhausted.

Standard Camouflage Colour (SCC 15). Introduced in April 1944 this colour was referred to as Olive Drab and was very similar to the US Army colour of the same name, the major difference was that it tended to fade to a greener shade

US Army No.9 Olive Drab. Tanks and other equipment received from the United States where painted in this colour and were not usually repainted unless absolutely necessary. It is almost certain that most Sherman tanks that were initially sent to France were painted in this colour. Vehicles returned for extensive repairs may well have been repainted with SCC 15 as would the 17pdr conversions. The Duplex Drive tanks employed on D-Day were all received directly from the US and there is no reason to suppose that they were not painted in US Army Olive Drab. I have found no evidence to support the contention that some tanks were camouflaged in a combination of one of these colours and SCC 14 Black, as lorries and cars were, during the Normandy fighting. Photographs clearly depicting disruptive patterns of camouflage applied to tanks all seem to have been taken much later.

Dragon Models Ltd
B1-10/F., 603-609 Castle Peak Rd.
Kong Nam Industrial Building
Tsuen Wan, N. T., Hong Kong.
www.dragon-models.com

Dragon USA
1315 John Reed Ct, City of Industry,
CA 91745, USA
www.dragonmodelsusa.com

Tamiya Inc
Shizuoka City, Japan
www.tamiya.com

Tasca/Asuka Model
www.tasca-shop.ocnk.net

Royal Model
Via E. Montale, 19-95030 Pedara, Italy
www.royalmodel.com

Italeri S.p.A.
via Pradazzo 6/b
40012 Calderara di Reno
Bologna, Italy
www.italeri.com

Jordi Rubio
Carrer de Còrsega, 625, 08025 Barcelona,
Spain
www. jordirubio.com/en/

Resicast
517 Vieux Chemin de Binche
7000 Mons
Belgium
www.resicast.com

Accurate Armour
Kelburn Business Park, Port Glasgow PA14
6TD, United Kingdom
www.accurate-armour.com

Eduard Model Accessories
Mirova 170, 435 21 Obrnice
Czech Republic
www.eduard.com

Hauler
Jan Sobotka
Moravská 38
620 00 Brno
Czech Republic
www.hauler.cz

Voyager
Room 501, No.411 4th Village
SPC Jinshan District
Shanghai 200540
P.R.China
www.voyagermodel.com

Aber
ul. Jalowcowa 15, 40-750 Katowice, Poland
www.aber.net.pl

E.T. Models
www.etmodeller.com

Friulmodel
H 8142. Urhida, Nefelejcs u. 2., Hungary
www.friulmodel.hu

Modelkasten
Chiyoda-ku Kanda, Nishiki-Cho 1-7, Tokyo,
Japan
www.modelkasten.com
Very difficult to navigate but worthwhile

Peddinghaus Decals
www.decals.guenstigergeht.net

Black Dog
Petr Polanka
Letecká 549
Libèice nad Vltavou
252 66, Czech Republic
www.blackdog.cz

Archer Fine Transfers
PO Box 1277
Youngsville, NC 27596
USA
www.archertransfers.com

ROCHM Model
www.rochmmodel.com
rochmmodel@gmail.com

Brach Model
Via Candia 23
10010 Barone Canavese,
Italy
www.brachmodel.it

Master Box
p.b. 4729,
Dnepropetrovsk
49094, Ukraine
www.mbltd.info

RB Model
Powstancow Wlkp.29B
64-360 Zbaszyn
Poland
www.rbmodel.com

M Workshop Singapore
91 Bencoolen St Sunshine Plaza01-58
Singapore
www.themworkshop.com

Tank Workshop
345 Wynbrook Dr
McDonough GA 30253
USA
www.tankworkshop.com

Dan Taylor Modelworks
55 Town Hill,
West Malling,
Kent, ME19 6QL
United Kingdom
www.dantaylormodelworks.com

Star/Bison Decals
Pershagsvagen
26:15139 Sodertalje, Sweden.
www.star-decals.net

Company B
www. Company-b-models-and-miniatures.myshopify.com

FURTHER READING

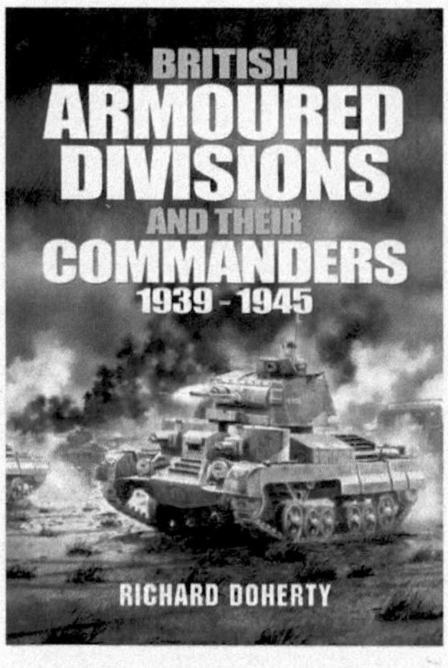

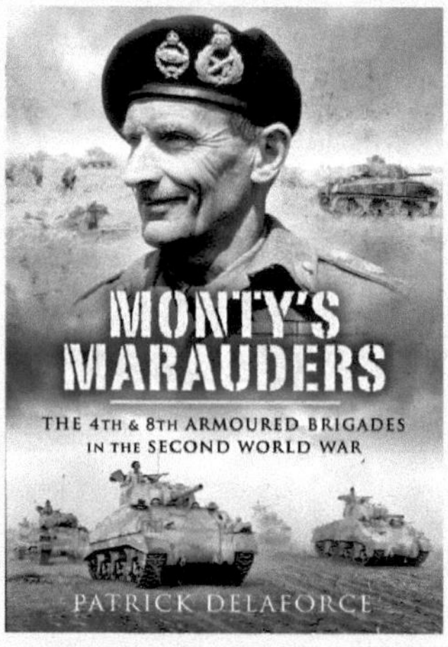

In compiling the unit histories and markings chapters I relied mainly on the works of B.T. White, William Platz and John Sandars. Although these authors are sadly no longer with us and their books were published some time ago, they are still the best references available. Over the years I have also compiled a great deal of information gleaned from memoirs and unit diaries which although far too numerous to mention here should be at least acknowledged. Most of the information in the technical section was taken from Sherman, A History of the American Medium Tank *by R.P. Hunnicutt, still regarded as the foremost authority on this tank. I also referred to my own previous works and the Sherman Minutia website, all of which owe a great deal to my old friend Leife Hulbert. All the illustrations were based on photographs of actual tanks and where I have been forced to speculate I have tried to make this clear. I would like to thank the modellers who graciously allowed me to publish the images of their work and Rupert Harding at Pen & Sword for his advice, assistance and above all patience. Of the product manufacturers I must make special mention of Roberto Reale of Royal Model, Sheng Hui of ROCHM, Jan Zdiarsky from Eduard Accessories and Freddie Leung of Dragon Models who all helped enormously. As always, I am indebted to Karl Berne, Valeri Polokov and J.Howard Parker for their invaluable assistance with the photographs and period insignia.*